The Family Guide to Point Reyes

A project to benefit the
Papermill Creek Children's Corner

Karen Gray

Chapter Plate Illustrations - Karen Gray
Book Design - Erica Elliott
Illustrations - Ane Roveta
Edited by Nancy Adess

CHARDON PRESS

First Edition, 1996. All Rights Reserved. No part of this book may be reproduced in any form or by any means without permission in writing from the publisher.

Cover illustration and chapter plate illustrations by Karen Gray
Additional illustrations by Ane Rovetta

Edited by Nancy Adess
Book and Cover design by Erica Elliott

Printed in the United States of America

Library of Congress Catalog Card Number: 96-083378
ISBN: 0-9620222-7-6

PRINTED ON
RECYCLED PAPER

5 4 3 2 1

DEDICATION

Every day when I leave my small son at the Papermill Creek Children's Corner, I am amazed. The director and teachers who so skillfully explain the seed pods gathered for the window sill nature display or the caterpillars transformed into butterflies about to be released into the flower garden by the children are the same people who change the dirty diapers, wipe the snotty noses and mop up the spilled paints—day, after day, after day.

And they do it all with grace, imagination and love. What's more, they are our neighbors, our co-workers in other places around town, and parents whose own children were in the school when it started years ago. They are our local treasures.

Suzanne D'Coney, my friend who helped in the production of this book, told me that when she first found out what her child's preschool teacher was paid, the information came as such a shock that she burst into tears. The people to whom we entrust our most precious beings, our future, our dreams, are paid so little that it shames me to read the school's budget every year.

Clearly these are people who work for love and not money. These are people who know the value of our little ones—priceless. They are people who teach for the joy of it. *The Family Guide to Point Reyes* is dedicated to them.

ACKNOWLEDGEMENTS

Papermill Creek Children's Corner is indebted to the generosity of a few people who helped in the publishing of *The Family Guide to Point Reyes.*

Dr. and Mrs. S. Friefeld are the parents of Wendy Friefeld, Director of the Children's Corner for over 12 years. The Friefelds gave in appreciation for the wonderful work done at the school.

Mr. and Mrs. Robert L. Gray are the parents of author Karen Gray and the grandparents of the Children's Corner alumnus Loren Elliott. The Grays share a heartfelt appreciation for the contribution that Papermill Creek Children's Corner makes to the lives of local families.

Lastly, an anonymous donor, friend to the author and Point Reyes community, offered financial help and invaluable encouragement when things got tough.

We are grateful to them all.

THE VISION FIRE OF
OCTOBER '95

The last plumes of smoke are fading from my view of the Inverness Ridge as I finish writing this book. My Point Reyes studio windows face west across the base of Tomales Bay to the ridgeline that defines the area south of Point Reyes Hill and Mount Vision. The Mount Vision Fire has burned more than 12,000 acres on the Point Reyes Peninsula. Roughly 14% of the Point Reyes National Seashore has burned.

People had kept the ridge from its natural cycle of forest fire and renewal for 50 to 100 years so that when the fire came it exploded with ferocity. Built up tinder and undergrowth caught in an instant after months of dry 'Indian Summer' heat. Winds picked up and for days fanned the fires beyond human control. Sadly, many people lost homes. Mercifully, no one was hurt.

The affect of the fire on the ecology of the area will be fascinating to see. As the report from the Point Reyes National Seashore "Vision Fire - October 14, 1995" observed, "The burn area is home to diverse plant communities, most of which have evolved over the millennia in response to periodic fire. The ecology has been affected more recently by the absence of fire through fire suppression efforts."

As the dry brush of the chaparral areas is cleared away by fire, spectacular displays of spring wildflowers generally occur. An ancient ridgetop resident, the bishop pine, bears cones that *require* fire to melt the resin that holds the cones closed and keeps the seeds captive until they fall on promising ground – open ground that is high in minerals and allows for sunshine to penetrate, just the conditions that follow a forest fire.

Wildlife is not always severely damaged by fire, either. As the Park Service report says, "Some have died, many have escaped, and competition for adequate food sources currently exists. Of greater importance is the preservation of the species. Fire plays a role in creating healthy, natural habitats for wildlife populations. Fire tends to burn in an uneven, patchy fashion. This creates a mosaic of diverse areas for wildlife – low green forage in recent burns, sheltering stands of brush and trees in unburned areas and standing dead trees that provide nesting cavities and insects for food.

The Seashore has suffered great loss, but it is not devastated. The cycle of life continues and regeneration will be evident in the long term."

The best overlooks for studying the fire zone are: Arch Rock, at the end of the Bear Valley Trail; Estero Trailhead, off of Sir Francis Drake Boulevard just past the Mount Vision turn-off; Bull Point Trail, off Sir Francis Drake Boulevard on the way to Drake's Bay; and Drake's Beach. Call the Bear Valley Visitor Center information number for updates on trails (415) 663-1092.

Table of Contents

Introduction   xiv

List of Chapter Plates by Karen Gray   xvi

List of Illustrations by Ane Rovetta   xvii

CHAPTER 1 -- GETTING READY: 1
        SAFETY, GEAR, ETIQUETTE & ATTITUDE

CHAPTER 2 -- GETTING YOUR BEARINGS: 9
        RESEARCH & EDUCATION CENTERS

Bear Valley Visitor Center, Point Reyes National Seashore
Ken Patrick Visitor Center, Point Reyes National Seashore
Point Reyes Lighthouse Visitor Center, Point Reyes National Seashore
Jack Mason Museum, Inverness
Audubon Canyon Ranch, Stinson Beach
Point Reyes Bird Observatory, Bolinas

"The Turkey Vulture and the Winter of '95" Story by Susan Brayton........20

CHAPTER 3 -- WHERE THE LAND MEETS THE SEA: 23
        THE BEAUTIFUL BEACHES

Perfect for Toddlers......................26
  Chicken Ranch Beach, Shell Beach, Heart's Desire Beach
Beaches for Bigger Kids 29
  Abbott's Lagoon, Kehoe Beach & McClure's Beach, Drake's Beach,
  Limantour Beach
Especially for Beachcombers......................38
  Millerton Point, Abbott's Lagoon, North & South Beach, Kehoe Beach

" Jellyfish" Story & Illustration by Ane Rovetta......................40

CHAPTER 4 -- HIT THE TRAIL! HIKING THE MAGICAL TERRAIN OF POINT REYES 43

Wheelchair Accessible and Rest Stop Trails....................................44
Bear Valley Trail, Earthquake Trail, Johnstone-Jepson Trail Loop,
Abbott's Lagoon Trail to the footbridge, Pierce Point Ranch Self-Guided
Tour, Estero Trail, Cross-Marin Trail, Five Brooks Stable and around
the Old Mill Pond, Stinson Beach Park

Hikes with Children in Jogger Strollers....................................58
Tomales Bay Trail, Tomales Point Trail, Estero Trail beyond the bridge,
Limantour Estero Trail, Muddy Hollow Trail, Coast Trail to Bass Lake
and Alamere Falls

Walks for Preschoolers...69
Millerton Point State Park, Bear Valley Trail, Woodpecker Trail,
Trail to Kule Loklo Indian Village and Morgan Horse Ranch,
Hagmaier's Pond

Hikes for Older Children...75
Audubon Canyon Trail, Griffin/Bourne Trail Loop, Fern Canyon
Trail and other trails

"A Shiny, Slimy Story" Story & Illustration by Ane Rovetta.................78

CHAPTER 5 -- SPECIAL PLACES IN THE PARK FOR CHILDREN 81

Kule Loklo Indian Village
Morgan Horse Ranch

"Wheezy, Breezy Wings" Story & Illustration by Ane Rovetta............85

Douglas Fir Grove with Acorn Woodpeckers
Pierce Point Ranch
Tule Elk Preserve
Point Reyes Lighthouse
Point Reyes and Tomales Point -- Gray Whale Migration

"Salmon Boy" Story by Jules Evens, Illustration by Karen Gray 92

Samuel P. Taylor State Park – Lagunitas Creek Salmon Run

CHAPTER 6 -- TOWN JOYS FOR KIDS 97

Dance Palace Community Center
Fire Trucks at Point Reyes Fire House
Calf Corrals at Giacomini Dairy
Moo Cow Clock

Tomales Bay Community Playground
... And Further Afield: The Rouge et Noire Cheese Factory and Pond,
Oysters on Tomales Bay

CHAPTER 7 -- GONE FISHIN': WHAT'S BITING & WHERE   103

Fishing License and Regulations, Study the Tides, Where to Get Gear
and Bait, Where to Go Surf Fishing and Lake Fishing

CHAPTER 8 -- MESSING ABOUT IN BOATS, KAYAKS,   111
              CANOES & INFLATABLES

"Mole goes boating with River Rat..."
  from Wind in the Willows *by Kenneth Grahame*...............................*112*
**Heart's Desire Beach, Limantour Estero, Papermill Creek at
White House Pool**..**113**

"Mole Takes the Oars..."
  from Wind in the Willows *by Kenneth Grahame*...............................*116*

"Osprey's Boldness" Story & Illustration by Ane Rovetta....................*117*

CHAPTER 9 -- JUST LOOKING: THE AMAZING   119
              TIDE POOLS
McClure's Beach, Chimney Rock..**121**

CHAPTER 10 -- WHERE TO SEE BEAUTIFUL SUNSETS,   123
               MOONRISES AND STARS
Looking Westward: Sunsets...**124**
  Kehoe Beach, Mount Vision, Estero Trail

Looking Eastward: Moonrises...**126**
  Tomales Bay Community Playground, L Ranch Road above
  Marshall Beach, White House Pool, Bolinas Ridge Trail

"Bat Shapes the World" Story & Illustration by Ane Rovetta..............*127*

What about the Stars?...131

Maybe You Can Have It All: The Sun, the Moon and the Stars!..........132
Tomales Bay Trail, EAC Elephant Mountain Hike, Tomales Point
Trail, Mount Vision - Piper on the Ridge

"Owl and the Sparkles" Story & Illustration by Ane Rovetta...............*134*

CHAPTER 11 - PICNICS & BARBECUES: 135
DINING WITH MOTHER NATURE

"Mole and Rat's Picnic..."
from Wind in the Willows *by Kenneth Grahame*....................................*136*
Barbecues...137
Millerton Point Park, Heart's Desire Beach, Heart's Desire
Campground, Bear Valley Picnic Grounds, Drake's Beach
Picnic Tables...139
"Turkey Vultures, The Soaring Untouchables,"
Story by Jules Evens...*141*

CHAPTER 12 - HORSEBACK RIDING & TREKKING   147
WITH LLAMAS

CHAPTER 13 - LIBRARIES & BOOKSTORES   151
Inverness Public Library
Point Reyes Public Library
Bookstore at Bear Valley Visitor Center
Bookstore at Ken Patrick Visitor Center
Bookstore at Lighthouse Visitor Center
Brown Study Books
Point Reyes Books

CHAPTER 14 - LOCAL MEDICAL CARE   157

CHAPTER 15 - FIELD TRIPS & CAMPOUTS   161

Audubon Canyon Ranch
Bear Valley Visitor Center -- Camping reservations and telephone for deaf
Camelid Capers
Footloose Forays with Michael Ellis
Marin County Naturalist Field Walks with Bob Stewart
Marine Mammal Center
Oceanic Society
"Point Reyes National Seashore: Events & Information"
        Published quarterly
Point Reyes Bird Observatory & Newsletter
Point Reyes Field Seminars
Samuel P. Taylor State Park Ranger Station
Tamalsaka Kayak Rental & Instruction
Tomales Bay State Park Ranger Station
Trailhead Rentals
Wildcare Terwilliger Nature Education Center & Wildlife
    Rehabilitation

YEARLY CALENDAR OF EVENTS   165

What to Do on a Rainy Day   173

FIELD NOTES

©1995 Ane Rovetta

INTRODUCTION

This book grew out of the questions from the many guests who stayed at my bed and breakfasts, Jasmine Cottage and Gray's Retreat. It was twelve years ago that I opened the first bed and breakfast cottage in Point Reyes. The cottages became places where people returned over the years to get to know this extraordinary area better. As honeymooners came back for anniversaries, eventually they brought along babies. As the children grew, the questions evolved from "Where can we go for a quiet, romantic stroll?" to "Where can we take our new infant for a picnic on the grass?" "Where can we swim with toddlers in Tomales Bay?" "Where can we get a fishing license to try out our daughter's new surf-casting rod?" or "Where should we rush our son?", who had fallen on a steep trail down to the beach.

My own family grew alongside those of my guests. I now have a small son who is my favorite companion in sharing the splendors of Point Reyes. First as a toddler and now as a preschooler, he is cared for during my work day by the teachers at the Papermill Creek Children's Corner. In a building realized through the volunteer efforts of many people in town, he is encouraged to learn how to be a part of his community while he is tutored in the wonders of the natural world—and his own part of it—beautiful Point Reyes.

These past few years have confirmed for me what I always knew was true here: the beauty and richness of the landscape are reflected in the community life. I live in that rare and fragile place where my grandparents, my parents and I grew up—the small town of rural California. It is a place of many blessings for those who live here, especially our families.

Papermill Creek Children's Corner is one of those blessings. I cannot imagine life in this town without it. Apparently I am not alone, for lots of people in town—and not just those with children—dedicate their time and money to keeping the school going.

If you have also been a part of this kind of effort in your own community, you know that once the long haul of grant writing, fund-raising and actual building is completed, the work is not over. The work is never over. Next comes the volunteer building maintenance, the landscaping, the weeding, building the play structures in the yards, the annual bingo nights and silent auctions, the pizza sales, more grant proposals, spaghetti feeds and clean-up days. I expect that my townspeople are unusual but not unique in their great willingness to forego personal leisure for the gratification of community service. I think this goes on in country towns, suburbs and cities all over America.

What is unique about Point Reyes is that my town sits at the edge of one of the jewels of the American Park System: The Point Reyes National Seashore. Our area also includes beautiful Tomales Bay State Park, the Golden Gate National Recreation Area, and thousands of acres of rolling pasture lands. This exquisite place is a "backyard" for myself and my friends who helped me write *The Family Guide to Point Reyes.* Many of us know it very well. Some of my friends have grown up here, or spent summers here, or lived and worked and played here for decades. Some are avid fishermen, some dedicated swimmers or boaters on the bay, some professional naturalists or historians of the area. I am happy to share our love and understanding of Point Reyes with your family.

This book, then, is intended to serve as a bridge between me and my family, and you and yours. It is also intended to become a bridge between our dreams for our children's school and their realization. The proceeds from the sale of *The Family Guide to Point Reyes* will help keep Papermill Creek Children's Corner open for our children, and maybe even our children's children.

Karen Gray
Point Reyes Station, California
February 1996

CHAPTER PLATES

by Karen Gray

CHAPTER 1:   Robin's Nest in Cotoneaster Branch
Speckled Eggshell Border

CHAPTER 2:   Brown Pelican
Eelgrass with Surf Perch Border

CHAPTER 3:   Baby on Heart's Desire Beach
Seashell and Eelgrass Border

CHAPTER 4:   Child Hiking Muddy Hollow Trail
California Newts and Stinging Nettle Border

CHAPTER 5:   Child Park Visitor with Ranger in Kule Loklo
Coast Live Oak Border

CHAPTER 6:   Child and Kid at Point Reyes Livestock Show

CHAPTER 7:   Fishing Children with Leopard Shark
Squid Border

CHAPTER 8:   Avocet on Beach
Kelp Border

CHAPTER 9:   Child in Sneakers at Tide Pool
Flotsam and Jetsam Border

CHAPTER 10:   Mother and Child Watching Moonrise Over Tomales Bay
Flying Bats Border

CHAPTER 11:   Great Blue Heron with Snake
Pacific Tree Frog, Dragonfly and Smartweed Border

CHAPTER 12:   Turkey Vulture with Bull Tule Elk Grazing
Wild Oats Border

CHAPTER 13:   Father and Child Seen Through Window of Library
Wildflower Border

CHAPTER 14:   Scarecrow with Crow
Pea Vine Border

CHAPTER 15:   Mother and Child Watching Raccoon in Campground
Pine Cone Border

ILLUSTRATIONS

by Ane Rovetta

Scrub Jay Taking Acorns from Basket...........xiii

White-Crowned Sparrows.................................2

Brush Mouse...3

Elephant Seal on Beach with Rocks................4

Rough-Skinned Newts.....................................5

Mountain Lion (Cougar)..................................7

Chipmunk with Nut..11

Harbor Seals on Beach with Cliffs........12 & 114

Bobcat.. 15

Lesser Tern Feeding Chic................................18

Hermit Crab and Kelp 24

Crayfish..27

Sea Shell...29

Sea Snail...31

Sea Lion..39

Jellyfish..40

Chipmunk in Leaves......................................46

Great-Horned Owl with Squirrel....................54

Banana Slug..56

Harvest Mouse...58

Cooper's Hawk...64

Acorn Woodpecker...66

Kestrals...77

Mating Bananna Slugs 78

Swallowtail Butterfly......................................85

Barn Swallows.. 86

Great-Horned Owl.. 88

Barn Swallows on Wire................................100

Goat..101

Dragonfly..104

Pair of Ospreys with Chicks in Nest............117

Sea snail...120

Large-Eared Bat..128

Saw-Whet Owl..130

Raccoon..132

Pair of Owls with Moon...............................134

Long-tailed Weasels.....................................138

Fox..140

Pacific Tree Frog with Shelf Fungus............148

Llama..149

Western Toad..152

Coyote with Moon..154

Dragonfly..173

Water Beetle...174

Robin's Nest in Cotoneaster Branch *Speckled Eggshell Border*
©1995 Karen Gray

Chapter 1

Getting Ready:
Safety, Gear, Etiquette & Attitude

GEAR & CLOTHING

Your time in Point Reyes will be more rewarding with some preparation. First, let's talk gear and clothes. Because the weather in Point Reyes is so variable, from morning to afternoon as well as day to day, everybody is well advised to dress in layers of clothing that can be added or removed as conditions change: cool shirts and pants with sweaters and hooded jackets to wear over them. Hats are a necessity, warm ones for the fog and wind, broad-brimmed ones for the sunshine. Sunscreen is essential also. The overcast on the coast can mislead you into thinking that the children won't get sunburned, but they will. Depending on the season, the day will move from cold and foggy in the morning to hot and sunny in the afternoon; then the cold winds begin to blow off the Pacific Ocean and later on the thick fog rolls in.

Be aware also that the Point Reyes area has such marked variations in local topography that the weather conditions can

©1995 Ane Rovetta

©1995 Ane Rovetta

change drastically within a few miles. Carry a day pack with a few layers of clothing and spare hats. Lightweight rain ponchos are a good idea in cooler weather - not necessarily for rain, but for the heavy fog drip that can leave you chilled to the bone before you get back to a heated space. Water bottles are another essential. Most of the trails in Point Reyes have no water and drinking from creeks is not safe. These days *Giardia* (among other bugs carried by people and other mammals) has been found in even the most remote mountain streams. Moleskin for blisters, dry socks, insect repellent for the warm mosquito months, and a basic first aid kit are all a good idea. A product called 'Technu' (for poison oak) is a smart addition to a standard first aid kit. (Look for it in any pharmacy.)

Carry a compass and show your older children how to use it. A whistle worn around each child's neck and a lesson in "hugging" a tree if lost are good beginnings for all children on hikes. Kids can be taught to stick by a tree if lost and blow their whistle at intervals until found by an adult.

Flashlights - one for each person - are a good idea as well. If you lose track of time and the fog rolls in it can get dark fast before you find your way back to the trailhead. If you give each child her own flashlight and teach her how to use it for signalling, she will be better equipped in case of getting lost.

Good trail maps for the entire Point Reyes area are available free of charge from the ranger's desk at the Bear Valley Visitor Center and at the other park visitor centers. Always carry one with you on unfamiliar trails.

SAFETY

There are several common threats in the Point Reyes landscape; two can be avoided with a little knowledge: *poison oak* and *stinging nettles*. Poison oak is prolific and dangerous if not respected from a distance. As if that weren't enough, it is expert at camouflage. Teach your children to recognize and avoid it. It may weave itself into the blackberry thicket and you may notice its shiny three leaves only after you have already reached in for that perfect berry. It grows creeping along like a groundcover in the windswept grasslands, nearly invisible - though still potent - when the stems are bare in winter. It may grow with large, sinewy, vine-like stems right up a Douglas fir tree for twenty feet, wrapping the trunk in beautiful fall color. Skin reactions to poison oak can be itchy, painful, and sometimes serious. Don't tangle with it!

People don't usually react to poison oak until 24 hours after they've been exposed. If you think you may have touched it, remove all your clothes as soon as you get home. Wash them in hot detergent with a little bleach added. Wash yourself in a <u>cold</u> shower with 'Technu' to help remove the offending oils from your skin. Poison oak is systemic with symptoms that can begin with itching and end in painful swelling and oozing lesions. My grandmother once breathed the smoke from a brush fire of poison oak and ended up in the hospital. Consult a doctor if your symptoms become serious.

Stinging nettles are seasonal, mostly limited to bogs and streamsides in the spring. They are usually dried up and gone by late summer. In wet years they can be three feet high and densely cover small meadow and wastelands. Skin brushed up against stinging nettle is immediately painful and brings up welts in the same way as an insect's sting. Fortunately, you carry the best antidote with you - fresh urine. The chemical in nettles that stings you is acid, urine is base, so you can neutralize the effect right on the spot.

Another remedy is *equesetum* or "horsetails," which conveniently grow in the same habitat. Slice open the stalk lengthwise and smear the clear silica gel from inside on

the stinging skin. It will neutralize the nettle's chemical and stop the stinging right away. Long pants, high socks, and long sleeves over bare arms are the best protection.

When I was a child in the San Joaquin Valley, we lived in my great grandparents' old place which had a large garden in the back with a patch of stinging nettle that grew every year. One season it was a rite of passage for all the kids who played in the area to run through the patch in shorts. We survived. Children may be quite uncomfortable for some minutes after brushing nettles, but the effect is temporary.

The third common threat is not so easily seen: *ticks.* Ticks are so common in the coastal chaparral that our wild mountain lilac (*Ceanothus thyrsiflorus*, "blue blossom") is also called "'tick brush." Ticks live in the brush and grasslands, dropping or climbing onto mammals (that's you) when the opportunity presents itself. Their mode of survival is to dig their head into the mammal's hide and suck its blood, eventually ballooning in body size as a result of its feast. It's a grisly way to make a living viewed from our perspective, but that's the ingenuity of Mother Nature for you.

If you find a tick attached to you, hold its body and twist it slightly while pulling gently outward to remove it. Be sure that the head comes out, too. (If not, you could have a doctor remove it.) Wash your hands well with soapy water.

©1995 Ane Rovetta

Ticks set up shop in your body rather than biting you and moving on like many other insects. Their bites can be uncomfortable and you run some risk of infection, as with any skin wound. However, the more serious risk is *Lyme disease.* Caused by a microscopic spirochete that gets into the bloodstream through the tick's bite, Lyme disease can bring on initial flu-like symptoms of fever, aching muscles, and a ring-like rash around the bite up to a month after your are bitten. Eventually, if untreated, the disease can be quite debilitating, producing arthritis.

Not all ticks carry Lyme disease. The tiny deer tick is the only native tick known to carry it, and only about 2% are estimated to be infected. But better safe than sorry, right? The deer tick is tiny (the size of a poppy seed or pinhead), reddish brown and not always apparent when it bites, since it is so small. If you find that someone in your family has been bitten by what may be a deer tick, save it and bring it to a local doctor within 72 hours for identification. Or, if after being out on the trails, one of you develops flu-like symptoms and/or a red rash on your body within 2 to 4 weeks, see a doctor right away.

For prevention, wear light-colored clothing, tuck your pant legs into your socks, wear high shoes or boots, and check everybody's body and clothes for traveling ticks at the end of a day's outing - especially the backs of neck, body creases, and belt line. Tick season tends to coincide with the onset of the rainy season, but they are around all the time in this temperate climate. Carry a lightweight tarp that you can lay out for everybody to sit on (or use your rain poncho) during your hiking breaks. Shake it out carefully and check each other's clothes when you get up. There are also tick repellents available in pharmacies and outdoor supply stores to spray on your boots and clothing.

ETIQUETTE

Cooperation and sharing the load are prerequisites for fun on an outing. Kids who learn early to carry their own weight are pleasant companions on the trail. My son started out with a small day pack when he was just 2 1/2 and proudly carried his own water, bug house for study, binoculars, flashlight, and lunch. Now he just assumes that he will carry his share like everybody else.

When returning from the beach or trail, don't bring souveniers from nature. Everything you find in nature has a place and is needed by everything else. The more we learn about the natural world the more we see how it is a complex tapestry with every thread important for the strength of the whole fabric. Nothing is unimportant in the natural landscape. Study it and leave it alone.

Except the litter. If you take a bag for garbage along with you, you can take out a little more trash than you brought in, doing Mother Nature a respectful service. We are all stewards of the land and collecting the litter that others thoughtlessly leave behind is a good way to begin acting like it.

The call of nature is unavoidable, often urgent with small children. If your family is away from restrooms and someone must urinate, take them at least 200 feet away from the trail or any water course. If they must defecate, take them the same distance and dig a six-inch-deep hole in which to bury the feces. Be sure to take any toilet paper out with you. It does not decompose rapidly in the ground.

ATTITUDE

There are wonderful things to see in Point Reyes. The interesting thing is what happens when you set out to see them. Once my family headed out the Tomales Point Trail from Pierce Point Ranch to see the magnificent *tule elk* in the preserve there. We had our binoculars for spotting. We were especially quiet so as not to scare them off. We hiked over hill and dale and never spotted a one. As we were dragging back, disappointed, in the dusk we saw her: a beautiful, sleek bobcat coming out for her nocturnal hunting foray. She was stunning.

At another time of year we drove out to the ranch with friends from Minnesota warning them all the way: "Yes, this is the tule elk preserve but we will be very lucky if we see one. There is no predicting Mother Nature." As we crested the hill and started down the road toward the ranch, there they were, whole harems of them, lounging magnificently in the grass on both sides of the road like placid dairy cows. We parked the car and quietly crept to within a respectful distance. They hardly looked in our direction.

After living in West Marin for eighteen years and longing for the sight of a mountain lion on every outing into the wilderness area, we were driving home one night from the movies. It was on Lucas Valley Road at about 10:30 - the biggest Afghan I'd ever seen. . .or was it a golden lab?. . .No, it was a pony loose from one of the the neighbor's corrals. . .We all whooped at once as the long, floating golden tail vanished from our headlights' narrow beam, "A mountain lion! A mountain lion! That was a mountain lion!"

Which all goes to show: Mother Nature can be a trickster. You just never can tell. But you can sure try to have your eyes open for whatever she decides to give you that day. Just stay loose and remember who really sets the agenda for the meeting.

©1995 Ane Rovetta

FIELD NOTES

Brown Pelican *Eelgrass and Surf Perch Border*
©1995 Karen Gray

Chapter 2

Getting Your Bearings:
Research & Education Centers

There are six education centers and museums described in this chapter. Except for the largest, the Bear Valley Visitor Center (which is open every day of the year except Christmas), each has its own seasonal and weekly hours. Call ahead to confirm any of the days and times mentioned here.

BEAR VALLEY VISITOR CENTER
AND ENVIRONS

• Water available • Wheelchair access • Restrooms • Picnic tables
• Good site for drawing and painting

DIRECTIONS: From Point Reyes Station, take Highway #1 south over the green bridge. Take an immediate right onto Sir Francis Drake Boulevard. Take the first left onto Bear Valley Road (beware of oncoming traffic; they are traveling fast and the curve is blind). In about 2 miles take a right at the sign marking "Bear Valley Headquarters - Point Reyes National Seashore." Follow the drive in about 1/4 mile to the large barn structure on the right and park. This is the Bear Valley Visitor Center. About 2 miles from Point Reyes Station.

A family visit to the Bear Valley Visitor Center is a good beginning for your time in Point Reyes. You will find park rangers trained in naturalist education who are there to answer your questions. There are life-like exhibits of Point Reyes animals in their home environments that children can study close up: *harbor seals, wading shore birds, fox, bobcat, raccoons, great blue herons, deer*, even a *badger*. There's a low table of mysterious objects found in Point Reyes for the kids to handle and learn to identify: elk antlers, whale baleen, a seal skull, turkey vulture feathers. Look up when you're there since much of what makes Point Reyes unique is its bird life and many individuals are perched or flying in the upper reaches of the visitor center's main room. Children can climb the stairs to the observation platform and practice using the spotting scope to observe the scene.

To get you oriented, a short film about the park is shown in the auditorium at regular intervals throughout the day. A running seismograph in a glass case records the movement of the earth 24 hours a day while an accompanying exhibit explains earthquakes. There is a good collection of books, maps and field guides for browsing or buying and comfortable couches set around the wood burning stove - a cozy place to be on a cold, rainy day when the rangers keep the fire stoked.

While you are there you can pick up the free color brochure and map of the Point Reyes National Seashore. There is also a free black and white trail map for the Seashore. It will give you specific distances as well as rules and information on who uses the trail (horses? mountain bikers? wheelchair accessible?).

This is also the place to ask about reserving a campsite for an overnight stay in one of the four campgrounds in the park. The rangers can describe the different sites, the access trails, and make recommendations for your family. No camp sites are drive-in. Every campground in the park must be reached on foot, by horse, or by boat.

Across the road from the visitor center is the old *Douglas fir* grove and picnic grounds. Magnificent trees, a few barbecues and picnic tables on the grass make this a very easy resting spot for families with small children. The grove is surrounded by a low, split-rail fence for safety. The place is a favorite with locals for children's birthday parties. There is plenty of room for games and the adjacent meadow is a good place to fly kites.

There are also a few picnic tables behind the visitor center that look out across the Morgan horse pasture. Kule Loklo, a recreation of a traditional Coast Miwok village, is a short hike up the hill to the north. The Morgan Horse ranch is up the hill by way of the paved road to the west (you can see the red barn and outbuildings from the visitor center). Rangers to answer your questions in advance of visiting can be reached by phone at (415) 663-1092.

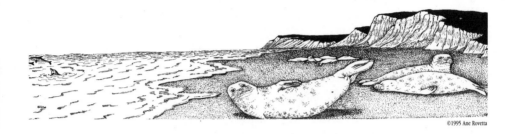

©1995 Ane Rovetta

KEN PATRICK VISITOR CENTER

• Water available • Wheelchair access • Restrooms
• Good site for drawing and painting • Food Concession

DIRECTIONS: Follow Highway #1 south out of Point Reyes Station. Take an immediate right onto Sir Francis Drake Boulevard just over the green bridge. Follow Sir Francis Drake Boulevard through the town of Inverness and over the hill. Bear left at the fork in the road, keeping to Sir Francis Drake Boulevard. Follow this out about 8 miles to the marked turn-off for Drake's Bay. The Ken Patrick Visitor Center is on the left. About 18 miles from Point Reyes Station.

The Ken Patrick Visitor Center at Drake's Beach is designed to teach all ages about the sea life and history of the Point Reyes Peninsula. A large seawater aquarium is richly stocked with local creatures from the coastal waters: *sea anemones*, gaudy *sea stars, eels, hermit crabs, sea urchins* and native fishes. There are rolling step stools and a railing for smaller children to see the aquarium at eye level. Ranger educators are on hand here also to teach you about Point Reyes. There is a *minke whale* skeleton suspended from the ceiling for study as well as an historical exhibit about the ships at Point Reyes, starting with the alleged landing here of Sir Francis Drake in 1579. A collection of books and guides emphasizing Sir Francis Drake, historical shipping and the migrating gray whale are for sale. There's a sunny corner with couches and windows that frame expansive views of Drake's

Bay and the Pacific. A beautifully preserved *brown pelican* is suspended in flight over the couch - perfect for close-up study of his bill and pouch.

Rangers to answer your questions by phone can be reached at (415) 669-1250. Ken Patrick is strategically placed so that after your family studies the local sea creatures, you can go right next door to the Drake's Beach Café and eat some.

POINT REYES LIGHTHOUSE VISITOR CENTER

• Water available • Wheelchair access to Visitor Center only (paved, nearly level road)
• Restrooms • Carry binoculars • Good site for drawing and painting

DIRECTIONS: From Point Reyes Station, take Highway #1 south over the green bridge. Take an immediate right onto Sir Francis Drake Boulevard. Follow Sir Francis Drake through the town of Inverness and over the hill (at the "Y" in the road, stay left). Through the dairy ranches, past the turn-offs for Drake's Beach and Point Reyes beaches North and South you go past the turn-off for Chimney Rock, clear to the dead end of Sir Francis Drake Boulevard (about 45 minutes from town). Park in the lot for the lighthouse and walk 1/8 mile to the visitor center and top of the stairs for the lighthouse. About 20 miles from Point Reyes Station.

As you walk to the end of the winding drive to get to the Point Reyes Lighthouse there is a white clapboard building that houses the visitor center. It sits at the crest of the point above the 300 steps that plummet down to the lighthouse and the sea. The lighthouse and the migration of the *gray whale* are the special features of this visitor center. Both are right there: the lighthouse way below seems to float out over the ocean. The gray whales, swimming near the coastline as they move along on their journey, actually have to chart their course out and around the lighthouse because the point juts so far out into the Pacific. For this reason it is possible to get quite close to the animals on especially lucky days. Most observation is improved by binoculars, so bring yours along or rent a pair for the day from Trailhead Rentals in Olema.

The rangers at the visitor center are specially trained to teach about the gray whales and to record the whales' yearly migrations from the Arctic Sea to Baja, Mexico and back again.There are books, guides, maps, posters and current log information about numbers of gray whale sightings posted in the visitor center. The months of January through March are best for viewing the gray whale migration. Weekends are very busy with limited parking. Call ahead for the shuttle bus schedule: (415) 669-1534.

The rangers can also give you details about the history of the lighthouse. If you descend the 300 steps to the lighthouse far below, you will be able to go across the bridge and stand right out on the lookout deck of the tower if you like. This is on calm days. Some days are so blustery on the point that the whole place closes to the public. You wouldn't be able to open your car door, anyhow. The weather out on the point can be wild. Fierce winds and bitter cold fog are common, even when the sun is shining in Point Reyes Station. Try to visit the lighthouse in the morning before the offshore winds begin to blow. Call ahead for weather information: (415) 669-1534.

JACK MASON MUSEUM

• Porta-potty • Picnic Table • Wheelchair accessible

DIRECTIONS: From the town of Point Reyes Station, follow Highway #1 over the green bridge. Take an immediate right onto Sir Francis Drake Boulevard and go about 3 miles to the village of Inverness. The second street on the left (both the first left and the second are called "Inverness Way") will take you to the museum in just one block. It's the yellow clapboard house with the white picket fence on the right, corner of Park Place. About 4 miles from Point Reyes Station.

The Jack Mason Museum is our local history museum. It is a room inside the building that houses the Inverness Library in Inverness. Founded by volunteers with the bequest of the residence of local historian Jack Mason, the museum houses rich and interesting exhibits, most often offering a presentation that is appropriate for all ages. For example, one recent photo exhibit documented "The Wonders of 4-H," chronicling the local children's involvement in raising animals with 4-H through four generations. Another chronicled the history of the wireless at Marconi Cove near Marshall. Another show explored the lives of ranchers' children in the last century with photographs and writing.

There is an archive attached to the museum for special research and a lovely cottage garden with benches and a picnic table. Volunteers who staff the library and museum are happy to answer questions or make referrals for you.

Jack Mason lived in the Point Reyes area most of his life. His various books about the area's history are available at the Inverness Library and the Point Reyes Public Library (in the little shopping strip next door to the local pharmacy at the corner of Highway #1 and 4th Street). These histories are out of print now. (Some are available for sale at Station House Gifts in Point Reyes Station.) The museum is open when the library is open on odd afternoons throughout the week and often on Sundays. Call for the taped message that will give you current exhibit information and hours: (415) 669-1099.

©1995 Ane Rovetta

AUDUBON CANYON RANCH

• Restrooms • Water • Picnic tables in meadow • Bookstore and museum
• Wheelchair accessible • Good view and sounds of rookery from ground at meadow

DIRECTIONS: From the town of Point Reyes Station head south over the green bridge on Highway #1. About 12 miles down, the road splits: the right leg goes to Bolinas, the left goes to Stinson Beach. Bear left, around the lagoon, for a mile and a half. You will see the signs for Audubon Canyon Ranch on your left. Turn in at the first driveway and proceed SLOWLY to the parking area. About 13 miles from Point Reyes Station.

Audubon Canyon Ranch sits in a sunny redwood canyon that opens onto beautiful Bolinas lagoon just a couple miles north of the seaside village of Stinson Beach on Highway #1. The *great blue herons* and *snowy egrets* of the region make their enormous stick nests in the branches of the high *redwood* trees, where the parents and chicks have a view of their fishing waters, Bolinas Lagoon.

Local conservationists' passion preserved the rookery and the lovely farmhouse that share the redwood grove. The sight of these magnificently graceful birds, whose wing spans reach seven feet, is a thrill for any age. The egret and heron parents fly back and forth from the lagoon bringing fish to their young all during the spring nesting season.

The ranch has carefully laid a trail up the canyonside through the *bay* and *oak* forest to a lookout just above the redwood grove. Here are benches for resting and spotting scopes for close-up observation of the mating pairs in their breeding plumage early in spring, and later, hatching eggs with young. All phases of their life cycle are fascinating. The birds first display their beautiful mating plumage to attract mates. Later in the season the racket from hatched chicks screaming to be fed echoes through the canyon. Eventually the exhausted parents get so sick of being harangued for food that they quit returning to the nest and the young birds they raised so carefully have to go out and find their own food.

The ranch opens to the public in mid-March and closes in mid-July. Weekday visits are by appointment only (lots of schools fill up the place with field trips then).

Weekends the ranch is open to the public (usually from 10:00 a.m. to 4:00p.m.) There are trained docents at the ranch who are available for tours and information about the bird colony. A beautiful museum with photos of the birds in all their phases - mating, plumage, nesting, hatchlings and fledglings - is across the meadow from the house. A book and gift shop on the property is carefully stocked to provide children information and inspiration about nature, most especially birds, of course. Audubon Canyon Ranch can be reached for information and reservations. Call ahead to schedule, (415) 868-9244.

NOTE: The ranch docents have an extensive program of naturalist education that takes them into the classrooms of Bay Area schools to teach children about Audubon Canyon Ranch. The school field trips usually follow. If you would like to arrange for docents to come to your school, call the ranch.

POINT REYES BIRD OBSERVATORY

• Restrooms   • Water   • Wheelchair accessible

DIRECTIONS: From the town of Point Reyes Station, head south over the green bridge on Highway #1 about 12 miles. Here the road splits. Bear right onto the Olema-Bolinas Road along the westerly side of the lagoon. At the first stop sign turn left toward the town of Bolinas. At the next stop sign, turn right and up the hill onto Mesa Road. Go 4 miles, following the signs to the bird observatory's Palo Marin Field Station. About 20 miles from Point Reyes Station.

Point Reyes Bird Observatory does research, policy development and training and education throughout a large part of the world. Drop-in visitors are always welcome at the field station without advance notice. The staff bands birds and gives demonstrations from May to November every day, and three times a week (Wednesdays, Saturdays and Sundays) from December to April. They close between noon and one for staff lunch every day. The banding demonstrations last for 1 to 2 hours. Birds are most active in the morning, so try to arrive early.

There are a number of displays in the visitor's center that are interesting for all ages and the staff is available to answer your questions about native birds and their environments. There is a self-guided nature walk nearby at the Arroyo Honda Creek. A small written guide is available. Duxbury Reef is close by if your family is interested in tidepooling (check your tidebook for times of low tides).

The drive to the field station from Point Reyes is beautiful, first winding through the pastoral Olema Valley, then past the Stuart Horse Ranch (foals and colts out in the pastures with their mothers in the spring), then along the Bolinas Lagoon and ending in the grasslands of Palo Marin.

The staff at the PRBO Palo Marin Field Station can be reached for information and hours at (415) 868-0655.

©1995 Ane Rovetta

FIELD NOTES

The Turkey Vulture
& the Winter of '95

The rain had been pouring for days and nights. In the evenings we snuggled by the fire, black dog close to the hearth, damp wood sizzling in the woodstove. At bedtime, the rain, unrelenting, splashed on the roof and the wind blew wildly around the house. Inside, the electric lights flickered on and off. On nights like these trees might fall on power lines and we could be plunged into darkness. Candles and flashlights were at the ready for we are often without electricity in the winter in Point Reyes.

Lying in my cozy bed, a hot water bottle at my feet, I was reminded of the winter of 1982, when Inverness and Inverness Park were isolated for days because of the January storm's disastrous impact: sliding mud closed the roads, towns were flooded, and whole houses, unable to withstand the fast-moving mud, slid downwards into Tomales Bay. We lived without electricity for several days and delved into our supplies of food and water which we had stored in case an earthquake occurred. Other disasters in California never seem so imminent as an earthquake. We were prepared for earthquakes, but in 1982 we were not prepared for the floods.

Now, after more than a decade of drier than usual winters, abundant winter rains at the end of 1994 were a welcome sight. We could leave behind the threat of forest and grassland fires for another year. The years of drought had ended and the hills were turning velvet green. Plants and trees were nourished. Streams gushed down to the Bay. In the early days of 1995, though, I was afraid this winter could bring a repeat of the 1982 flooding. With the force of this January storm, nighttime dreams were interrupted into wakefulness. In the morning, it was with relief we saw that repairs made to creeks and ditches in our valley after 1982 had held.

But there can be no preventive methods to aid wildlife when the rain pours. The small birds suffer greatly in wet and cold winters, and many die of hypothermia. This winter, for the Anna's Hummingbirds we hung feeders filled with sugared water on trees. Their nectar sources from the flowers had been dashed to the ground. Sopping wet Pine Siskins, tiny birds which are usually nervous of human habitats, ravenously devoured seed as I placed it in the birdfeeder. They swarmed around me like bees, landing on my arms, acrobatically taking the seed from my fingers, wet feathers sticking to their fragile bodies.

Within a couple of days, satiated and strong again, they had disappeared into their private world in the woods.

Early on this January morning, I looked out of my bedroom window and was relieved to see the rain, which had lashed down all night, had finally stopped. Ominous black clouds hung low in the sky and more rain was to come, though. I went downstairs intending to take my dog for her morning run, but just as I was about to open the kitchen door, I stopped in my tracks as I saw the evergreen hedge against the fence shaking vigorously in an otherwise still garden. The intermittent strong winds of the night had dropped. Why would the hedge be moving in such an agitated way, I asked myself. Was it a cat? Instinctively, I pulled the dog back into the kitchen. I stepped out cautiously and was startled to see the shape of what looked like a large animal teetering on the thin clumps of branches. I moved closer and recognized a Turkey Vulture. It is very unusual for a Turkey Vulture to land somewhere as domesticated as a garden! Had it spotted a dead animal in our bedraggled yard? I had never seen this bird so closely before. Its huge wings were thrashing helplessly. It obviously could not fly and was confused.

Fearing my presence, the large bird managed to heave itself from the hedge to the top of the garden fence and then drop with a thud to the other side and out of my view. Still curious, I carefully opened the garden gate and stepped quietly towards the bird's hiding place. As I observed, it turned wary eyes in my direction, then quickly looked away, as if by ignoring me it could eliminate my uninvited presence altogether. I was in awe of the close contact I had with this bird. I had witnessed vultures flying high above my house heading for their nighttime roost, or perched on top of a dead tree branch drying their wings. Sometimes I had startled a Turkey Vulture while driving my car and had seen it withdraw its red head from the carcass of an animal killed on the road and slowly fly away. These birds are not known to stay in close proximity to live mammals like myself. I had never been as close to a vulture as this. I was entering into the silent, private vulture's life and the vulture was entering mine in an unexpected way. Being so near to each other seemed to narrow the gap between our species. We were simply two earth creatures coming together by happenstance on a California winter morning. I shook myself from this revery. The bird was making no effort to move, and I knew it needed help. I could make a phone call, the bird couldn't.

I returned to the house. After a few calls my search for help led me to WildCare, the center for wildlife in Marin County. On their advice, I called the Marin Humane Society, which picks up animals in distress, whether domestic or wild. I was told to stand by until I heard from the Animal Rescue unit van. The call came and a man's voice asked me to give a running commentary on the bird's current condition. I could see the Turkey Vulture from where I stood as I talked on the kitchen telephone. By this time it had managed to get from the tree stump next to the shed to the top of the fence again. I told him the bird was wobbling back and forth looking as if it could topple over. He said the problem was the bird's wings were so saturated with water, they were too heavy to lift and fly. If rain occurred within an hour, the Turkey Vulture would be in deep trouble. The wings would be heavier still. It would be weak without food and possibly close to death, and who knows how long it had been grounded before I discovered it. He told me to call him if it rained again and he would come immediately and pick up the bird.

Blessedly, it didn't rain. But the clouds continued to hang low. Another storm was on its way. My elderly mother and I watched from an upstairs bedroom window, each with one eye on the Turkey Vulture, the other eye on the weather. Occasionally we used binoculars to get a closer look at the bird. It hopped a few feet along the fence, testing its huge wings. The wings were still too heavy to spread out and dry, and they flopped down close to its scrawny body. It lost its balance, and its weakened claws clutched clumsily for the safety of the top of the fence, wings glued to its sides. After many attempts, the Turkey Vulture was able to stretch out its wings to dry. It poised itself with more confidence, wings spread in wide splendor, head thrust forward, adjusting its balance more easily now. Drying time passed slowly. I left to do some chores and take the dog for her long-delayed walk from another exit, but often returned to the window to observe.

Four hours after my discovery in the hedge, wings dry now, opened and ready for flight, the Turkey Vulture lifted off the fence and lightly ascended. We watched as it circled around the house a few times, flapping and tipping its wings in harmony with the wind. Then it rose higher, joining a flock of Turkey Vultures soaring above, eventually becoming indistinguishable among the other vultures against the grey sky.

Baby on Heart's Desire Beach *Seashell and Eelgrass Border*
©1995 Karen Gray

Chapter 3

Where the Land Meets the Sea:
The Beautiful Beaches

The Point Reyes beaches are varied and wonderful. There are wild, dramatic beaches on the Pacific coast side of the Point Reyes Peninsula. There are placid, protected warm-water beaches for wading and swimming on the Tomales Bay side, as well as a few lesser known, protected beaches on the eastern shores of Tomales Bay, north of Point Reyes Station.

Mornings tend to be the most peaceful on the beaches since the afternoon winds come off the ocean fairly regularly. The summer weather pattern is one of fog in the morning burning off in the afternoons, so the sunshine often comes with the wind. The fall, though, tends to give you the best beach weather of all: warmest bay waters, clear mornings and a minimum of wind. "Indian summer" here follows the pattern for the rest of the greater Bay Area with the hottest days of the year often occurring in the months of September and October.

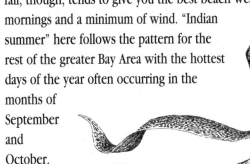

©1995 Ane Rovetta

Be familiar with the area's wind patterns: blowing hard off the ocean from the west and down Tomales Bay from the northwest; that way you can gauge the beach to visit that will be most sheltered and still provide the most sunshine (if it should decide to shine at all that day).

Regardless of the weather, Point Reyes beaches are always an adventure, with a rich array of wildlife, plant life, and plenty of flotsam and jetsam for play. 'Flotsam and jetsam' now refers to all the various debris that washes up onto the beach at high tide, natural and unnatural. In earlier times, 'flotsam' was any portion of a ship's cargo left floating on the water after a shipwreck, (get it? 'flot' for "float?'). This was all fair game for the locals on the beaches to gather up and claim ("finders - keepers, losers - weepers"). The 'jetsam' was any valuable cargo that had been jettisoned off the ship's side before a wreck in an attempt to lighten the ship's load and prevent sinking. Although today there is very little treasure washing up on the beaches in Point Reyes there are still shipwrecks off the dangerous rocks at the point, and a good deal of interesting 'f and j' does show up on our beaches - especially in the winter after a really good storm at sea.

Winter beachcombing is a local past-time that yields wonderfully unpredictable things. This beggar's treasure of potential artist's, architect's and playground supplies is great fun. The long, rubbery ropes of kelp make wonderful jump ropes. The driftwood is good for building structures. The jelly fish, dead birds, fish and seaweed are fascinating for study, drawing or painting. The bleach bottles, plastic floats, bits of fish net and whatnot are great for sculptures and play.

I once approached a distant family seated together around a driftwood table at the base of the cliffs on Kehoe beach. On closer inspection, as I got further down the beach, I could see that they were made of foam drums, seaweed 'hair,' old ropes and other objects scavenged along the tide line. I suppose the family sat there for days enjoying their repast, until the next stormy high tide took them apart and back into the sea.

P E R F E C T   F O R   T O D D L E R S

All the beaches in this section are sheltered coves on the western edge of Tomales Bay. They fall within the boundaries of Tomales Bay State Park, administered by the State of California. There are no open fires allowed on any of the beaches. Barbecues are provided at Heart's Desire Beach only. No dogs are allowed on any of the state park beaches.

CHICKEN RANCH BEACH

• Carry water • Porta-potties • Good site for drawing and painting

DIRECTIONS: From the town of Point Reyes Station, take Highway #1 south over the green bridge. Make an immediate right turn onto Sir Francis Drake Boulevard continuing through the village of Inverness. About a mile past the town, after you pass the yacht club, start looking for the large pullout on the right where the road curves broadly to the left. If it is a sunny day there will be a cluster of cars parked here in front of the willow trees that block your view of the beach. About 6 miles from Point Reyes Station.

I guess there must have been a chicken ranch here at some time but you'd never guess it now. This is a traditional favorite with locals and maintained by the Inverness Association, a local volunteer civic group. Please be especially careful to park well off the road without blocking the trail access and pick up your litter when leaving.

Chicken Ranch is the southernmost beach on Tomales Bay and loved for its warm shallow water, easy access and beautiful sweeping views of the hills to the east and south (Black Mountain, Mount Barnaby, Mount Tamalpais).

Because of its location, this beach is often in sunshine while those further out toward the ocean are socked in with fog. It is not, however, very sheltered from the winds that blow down the bay, so consider the conditions and place your bets. Water booties are a good idea since the soft sand turns to sharp granite rocks just a short way out.

SHELL BEACH

• Carry water   • Pit toilets   • Good site for drawing and painting

DIRECTIONS: From the town of Point Reyes Station, take Highway #1 south over the green bridge. Make an immediate right turn onto Sir Francis Drake Boulevard. Go through the town of Inverness to the base of the ridge, about 3 miles. Just past a place on the right marked "Sandy Cove" take a hairpin right turn up Camino del Mar. Stay to the right all the way past the signs reading "not a through road" and "no exit" to the small parking lot at the end. From here it is a quarter-mile walk down the steep switchback trail to the beach. About 8 miles from Point Reyes Station.

Shell is another of the Tomales Bay State Park beaches on the western side of Tomales Bay. Because it is not reached through the main entry for Tomales Bay State Park, it is one of the lesser known beaches on the bay. The trail winds steeply through a lovely woods of *bay* and *oak*, with *western sword fern, huckleberry, salal,* and, in the spring, *forget-me-nots.*

This cove is small and protected from winds. The sandy bottom is hospitable to bare feet. There is also a floating raft anchored out. Some overhanging trees provide shade at either end of the beach. It is narrow and loses the sun early in the day, so try to arrive early.

There is a "Shell Beach #2" over the trail to the north. However, local custom holds that this is a serene spot for those seeking a quiet read, a sun bath in the nude, or an intimate moment uninterrupted by the exuberance of little people. I used to be one of those folks (I may even be one again, some day) so I respectfully request that your family honor the custom.

©1995 Ane Rovetta

HEART'S DESIRE BEACH

• Water available • Wheelchair access • Restrooms with showers • Barbecues
• Good site for drawing and painting

DIRECTIONS: From the town of Point Reyes Station, take Highway #1 south over the green bridge. Make an immediate right turn onto Sir Francis Drake Boulevard. Drive through the town of Inverness. About three miles along the road splits in a 'Y'. Bear right onto Pierce Point Ranch Road. A couple miles down, take a right at the sign marking "Tomales Bay State Park - Heart's Desire Beach." Continue on down to the beach parking area, following the markers. About 12 miles from Point Reyes Station.

Heart's Desire Beach is one of those idyllic spots on Earth that bring other idylls to mind. In full summer regalia - colored beach umbrellas, floating kayaks, bright beach pails everywhere, toddlers wobbling to the water's edge for the first time hand-in-hand with a big person - it reminds me of a beach on the southern coast of France. With local Latino families often picnicking or celebrating birthdays at the barbecues it also reminds me of coastal villages in Mexico. The soft sounds and the small scale of the place combine with the bucolic view across the bay to give the entire scene a story book quality of utter delight.

For true relaxation and a peaceful time together, Heart's Desire is an abiding blessing for families. The sand is soft enough for tiny feet; there is some shade under the overhanging trees on the cliffs; the beach is small enough that you won't lose sight of your dashing children. There always seem to be enough kids of the right age for getting to know and sharing play. People treasure the beauty and quiet of this beach so there is a cozy, friendly feeling to the place.

This beach has all the extras that make hauling family provisions easy because you can drive up and park very near to the picnic area. There are restrooms with showers and sinks, low faucets for washing sandy children, wheelchair access to the restrooms and the picnic area, and a sandy cove sheltered from wind. The water is shallow for quite a ways out although water booties are a good idea for the rocky bottom at low tide.

In the summer and fall, early morning is a good bet since this eastern-facing cove gets the first morning sun rising over Elephant Mountain in Point Reyes Station. The sun goes down early behind the cliffs to the west so be warned: if you are here in the spring or fall when days are shorter you may lose the sun on the beach by mid-afternoon. The cove is cordoned-off with buoyed rope to protect swimmers from motor boats.

If you have left the kitchen sink at home, you can walk up the trail to the north through the woods about a quarter mile and set up on Indian Beach. Here there is a bark house built by volunteers in the old style of the Coast Miwok Indians who lived on the beach in the summers in the old days. It is used for educational workshops by the park rangers to teach about the Coast Miwok way of life and to tell their stories. There is also a freshwater creek with a footbridge spanning it. From here you can look for bat rays swimming in the shallow water below.

BEACHES FOR BIGGER KIDS

All these beaches are administered by the Point Reyes National Seashore. The Pacific Coast beaches are larger, more dramatic, and wilder than the protected shores of Tomales Bay. Heavy surf, sneaker waves, undertow and rip-tides are all possible hazards at the ocean side. Teach your children to pay attention to the warning signs and explanatory notes provided by the park at each site. None of these beaches except Drake's are possibilities for swimming. Swim at your own risk.

NOTE: When warned to check the tides for safety on particular beaches, be sure to notice the correction tables in the front of the tide book. The book is gauged to the mouth of the Golden Gate and tides in Point Reyes can vary from the printed time by an hour or more.

©1995 Ane Rovetta

ABBOTT'S LAGOON

• Carry water • Check tides • Dangerous surf and sneaker waves • Undertow
• Restrooms at trailhead • Carry binoculars and hand lens

DIRECTIONS : From the town of Point Reyes Station take Highway #1 south over the green bridge. Make an immediate right onto Sir Francis Drake Boulevard. Drive through Inverness and up the hill. Bear right at the "Y" in the road onto Pierce Point Ranch Road. Follow it out through the ranch lands to the marked trailhead for Abbott's Lagoon on the left. About 15 miles from Point Reyes Station.

The trail out to Abbott's Lagoon offers a great beginning for little hikers: nearly level all the way with lots of interesting flora and fauna and a beautiful footbridge over the creek when you reach the lagoon (in about 2/3 of a mile). The trail winds through pastureland with dense patches of *bush lupine* on rolling hills. The views are open for spotting *golden eagles, red tailed hawks, American kestrels, black-shouldered kites, northern harriers* ('marsh hawks') and other birds of prey that hunt here. My husband was out on this trail once at dusk and watched from behind a bush as a mother bobcat taught her cub to stalk rodents in the grass.

Once you reach the lagoon the landscape changes dramatically. The smooth gray water together with the white hills of fine sand make for a dreamlike quality. This is especially true on foggy days when the pearly cotton in the air blends with the shades of gray in the water and sand while the sound is muffled so that everything is softer to your eyes and your ears. If you stop to listen carefully, you will hear the hard surf of the Pacific crashing on the beach from over the high dunes some ways off.

The lagoon is a resting and feeding place for large numbers of water birds in the migratory seasons (spring and fall). Ducks of many kinds can often be seen congregating in large numbers.

Abbott's Lagoon is closed to the ocean much of the year by a seasonal sandbar. The bar breaches in heavy winter storm surges. This volatile mix of changing fresh and salt water makes for interesting variations in the plant life and the animals that visit the lagoon.

If you walk to the right around the lagoon, you will come over the rise to a view of the beach and the Pacific. This beach gets the full force of winter storms, so it is dramatically sculpted by winter weather fronts. During the winter months the sea offers up all kinds of junk treasures for play. Driftwood comes in every size with varied histories: lost logs from lumber mills up north, shattered pieces of shipwrecks, coconuts from Mexico, dead sea birds for study - the works.

©1995 the Rovetta

KEHOE BEACH

• Carry water   • Carry binoculars   • Check tides   • Dangerous surf
• Restrooms at trailhead

DIRECTIONS: Head south on Highway #1 from Point Reyes Station. Just over the green bridge, take an immediate right onto Sir Francis Drake Boulevard. Go through the town of Inverness and over the ridge. Bear right at the fork in the road onto Pierce Point Ranch Road. The turnoff for Kehoe Beach is just past the trailhead for Abbott's Lagoon on the left. About 18 miles from Point Reyes Station.

As with so many of our Point Reyes beaches, getting there is half the fun. Kehoe Beach is reached by a quarter-mile hike over rolling ground through fields of *yellow* and *lavender bush lupine*. A little creek and marsh are down on your left, alive with birds that nest in the tules: *red-winged blackbirds, wrens, yellow throats; egrets,* and *herons* feed here. There are ducks in the winter in the open water near the beach. Up on your right is the hillside pasture, populated by dairy cows that come right down to the trail - perfectly comfortable with your presence.

WARNING: On this trail, as well as others in the Point Reyes area, be respectful of the dairy cows and they won't bother you. Remember that they were here first. Many of the dairy ranches go back a hundred years. Never shout or frighten a cow - she could loose her milk, an expensive proposition for the rancher. Be aware of youngsters and be careful not to put yourself between a young calf and its mother. Last, beware of entering a pasture with a bull in it. They are the ones with the massive necks, horns and large testicles. They do not believe in sharing pastures. They may protect them and their cows with bull-headed ferocity. You may not be welcome.

When you reach Kehoe Beach you will see that it is broad and inviting. Lots of shorebirds work the tideline together here - *godwits, plovers, sanderlings, sandpipers* - all moving along the wet sand in some instinctive choreography, drilling down for the small animals left behind after the last wave.

The dunes are a fine shelter from winds, for resting and for picnics.

The cliffs up the beach to the north are interesting, offering small waterfalls in winter after a hard rain. My toddler son once found a rough-skinned newt at the bottom of a waterfall here. The newt must have slipped from the cliff top in heavy rains. Reckoning that the animal was not well-adapted to a saltwater environment we carried him back up the trail and let him go in the marsh.

In the springtime the bluffs above Kehoe Beach host a dense carpet of wildflowers: *California poppies, baby blue eyes, lupine, buttercups, tidy tips, pussy ears, forget-me-nots, indian paint brush, yarrow, sea asters, fiddle neck, blue-eyed grass, Douglas iris, yellow mustard* and *wild radish.*

MᶜCLURE'S BEACH

• Carry water • Carry binoculars • Check tides • Dangerous surf • Sneaker waves
• Undertow • Restrooms at trailhead

DIRECTIONS: From the town of Point Reyes Station follow Highway #1 south. Just past the green bridge, take an immediate right onto Sir Francis Drake Boulevard . Follow Sir Francis Drake through Inverness and over the hill. When you reach the "Y", bear right onto Pierce Point Ranch Road. Follow the road clear out to the end, passing Pierce Point Ranch just before the road dips down to the trailhead for McClure's. About 22 miles from Point Reyes Station.

McClure's Beach is the northernmost beach in the Point Reyes National Seashore. It's a good forty minute drive from town - but what a drive! You skirt the *bishop pine* forest that borders the Tomales Bay State Park before coming out into rolling, open pasturelands on both sides. From here you can see the Pacific Ocean ahead and Tomales Bay on your right. You will wind through dairy farms and then notice a high fence that glides out over the landscape in both directions with a break across the road for a cattle grate. This is where the cow territory ends and the *tule elk* preserve begins. Be on the lookout for these magnificent beasts. The males have impressive racks worn like oversized crowns on their heads.

As the road begins to wind down to the sea, you will notice a large pull-out and visitor information plaque on your right. A walk out to this promontory is rewarding. The broad view is remarkable and the annotated map does an excellent job of explaining the surrounding geography. From here, on a clear day, you can see northwest all the way to *Mount St. Helena* above the Sonoma Valley. You can see to the south and west are *Mount Tamalpais, Mount Barnaby* and *Elephant Mountain* here in Marin. You also get a very clear view of Tomales Bay as it marks the *San Andreas Fault Line* running through West Marin before it goes out to sea in the north and into Bolinas Lagoon in the south.

Here, also, you stand a good chance of spotting an *elk* harem or maybe a collection of young males waiting for their next chance to prove their strength over an old bull and enjoy the company of the females. The road makes its final big sweep as it passes Pierce Point Ranch. The dirt trail leading from the trailhead down to the beach is fairly steep, cut into the hillside bordering the creek that flows down and across the beach below. Once down to the beach (about a quarter mile) you will see very high, dramatic cliffs and rich rock outcroppings for tidepooling in minus tides. Down the beach to the south at low tide there is an opening in the rock wall that flows into the sea. You can scramble through this trough and come out onto an isolated little cove that is both sheltered from winds and sunny, as it faces due south. This is also a terrific place for climbing over the rock formations. **(Watch the tide and return to the main beach before the sea closes off the access. Beware of heavy surf and sneaker waves.)**

 WARNING: If you go to any of the Point Reyes beaches (but most especially McClure's) in the wintertime, when there may be storms out at sea, never turn your back on the ocean. Sneaker waves do come in here and can sweep an unsuspecting person off the rocks in a flash. Always be mindful that the ocean is a changing, unpredictable force that can harbor danger.

DRAKE'S BEACH

• Water   • Prepared Food • Picnic Tables   • Visitor center
• Showers   • Restrooms • Wheelchair accessible

DIRECTIONS : From the town of Point Reyes Station take Highway #1 south over the green bridge. Make an immediate right onto Sir Francis Drake Boulevard. Follow Sir Francis Drake through Inverness and over the ridge. Bear left at the "Y," keeping to Sir Francis Drake Boulevard. Follow this through the ranch lands to the marked turnoff for Drake's Bay and the cafe on your left. About 18 miles from Point Reyes Station.

A good 45 minute drive from Point Reyes Station, Drake's Beach is worth the trip because of the wonderful cafe, the terrific Ken Patrick Visitor Center, and a long expanse of beach sheltered from the prevailing winds on Drake's Bay. If it is a blustery day, the parking lot and entry area are wind tunnels, but don't let that fool you. Walk down to the beach and take a right heading west. You will soon be sheltered by the high cliffs that are now between you and the Pacific Ocean to the west.

 WARNING: Don't settle down right at the base of the cliffs - they are notoriously unstable. People have been killed by falling boulders.
Also, Snowy Plovers nest along this stretch of beach. Their nest is a shallow depression in the sand and very vulnerable to disturbance. Watch your step, especially in spring.

Locals report that boogie boarding and surfing are good here. All of these folks wear wet suits. The water is cold (although tolerable in a hot September). This is also an excellent spot for flying kites. You can move up and down the beach, depending on how windy the conditions are, and do very well maneuvering kites on the thermals rising up along the cliffs. Surf fishing is often good here, too.

If you don't want to be bothered with packing a picnic, Drake's Beach Café serves everything from a cup of clam chowder and a good burger to a wonderful fried oyster plate with green salad. It is a local favorite for breakfast on weekends. There are a cozy fireplace and tables inside with beautiful views - a lovely place to relax if the weather is stormy. Picnic tables are placed right at the dunes with a view of the bay for dining outside on warm days. This is the only food concession within the National Seashore.

LIMANTOUR BEACH

• Carry water (faucet at the trailhead) • Carry Binoculars • Check tides • Undertow
• Dangerous Surf and Sneaker Waves • Restrooms at Trailhead and Campground

DIRECTIONS: From the town of Point Reyes Station, take Highway #1 south over the green bridge. Take an immediate right turn onto Sir Francis Drake Boulevard. Take the first left onto Bear Valley Road (being careful of the oncoming traffic from around the blind curve). After a quarter mile, take the first right at the sign for Limantour Beach. Follow Limantour Road all the way to the end and park in the parking lot. About 8 miles from Point Reyes Station.

Limantour Beach is an easy drive from town. You wind through the ancient *bishop pine, oak* and *bay* forest of the ridge to come out into the open chaparral that rolls down to the sea. From the parking lot at the end of the road you take the paved, nearly level path over to the dunes. The path crosses Limantour Estero, giving you a close-up look at the ducks and other water fowl that use the estero for stop-overs. *Cattails, pickleweed, sea lavender, brass buttons* and *blackberry* thickets form a plant tapestry for nesting birds and other animals.

If you take the dirt path to your right just before the dunes, you will walk along the edge of the estero in the direction of its outlet to the sea. At the edge of the spit there are often *harbor seals* hauled out resting or, in the spring, having their pups here. Be especially quiet and do not leave the trail to approach them. They are easily disturbed, especially during pupping season. In winter you may be blessed with the sight of a flock of stark *white pelicans* spending the cold months by the sea before heading inland to fresh - water lakes to breed in spring. This walk just disappears in the dunes. It is what remains of the entry road for a planned subdivision of beach houses narrowly averted by the purchase of the land for the national park years ago. As you walk along in this precious stretch of nature you can remember the many volunteer conservationists who lobbied the government tirelessly to protect this beautiful coastline for us all.

Once my family and I were walking along the estero's edge, studying the interesting plants and objects that had washed up along the waterline. Under the surface there was a brightly colored creature that looked to have come from another planet. Clad in gaudy green, fuchsia, blue and yellow, this spectacular animal appeared in our field guide labeled as a *nudibranch* or - more humbly - a "sea slug." "Slug" hardly fit the flashy critter who glided along before us. None of us had ever heard of such an exotic animal. The thrill of stumbling on this one was tremendous. We were especially delighted to study it at leisure since - unlike so many wild animals confronted with humans - it's locomotion was very slow, sluggish even. What a treat!

If you walk straight over the dunes from the paved path, you enter Limantour Beach. There are lovely little hollows in the dune grass for shelter from the wind. The walks in both directions are wonderful. To the north you can go for more than a mile with a view of the white cliffs of Drake's Beach off in the distance. To the south the dunes give way to high cliffs and the beach ends eventually in sea-worn rock outcropping that host colonies of tideline creatures: *mussels, barnacles, sea star, anemone, periwinkles* and *hermit crabs*.

Coast Camp, one of the hike or ride-in campgrounds of Point Reyes, is near these rocks, marked by the enormous solitary *eucalyptus* tree above the trail up from the beach. It was planted as part of the old dairy ranch that is long gone. Now there are improved camp sites with outhouses and a faucet that runs potable water - if you don't mind the rotten-egg taste and smell of sulphur, that is. (Camp sites in the park are all by reservation only - up to 2 months in advance; so call ahead to Bear Valley Visitor Center if you want to spend the night.)

NOTE: There is poison oak on both sides of the trail up to the campground. The colonies of grasses on the dunes on all of Point Reyes' beaches are important habitat. If you do walk up into the dunes, be aware of the paths already established and do not trample any vegetation. Dunes are constantly shifting and the plants that settle there have a hard job of hanging on against weather and foot traffic. A good rule of thumb: if there is no clear path, stay off.

 *UPDATE: The Limantour area burned in October of 1995. Watch for spectacular wild flower displays in the spring and dramatic changes in vegetation.*

ESPECIALLY FOR BEACHCOMBERS

MILLERTON BEACH

• Carry water • Restroom at trailhead • Picnic tables

DIRECTIONS: Heading north out of Point Reyes Station on Highway #1 you wind up the road about 5 miles. Pull in where the sign marks "Tomales Bay State Park - Millerton" at the entry to a grove of eucalyptus trees with an old barn. Park in the lot and walk over the footbridge to the south to get to the beach, or over the trail straight ahead to traverse the bluff overlooking the bay.

This cozy cove faces due south for sunshine and is remarkably sheltered from the winds, even when it is blustery everywhere else. Beach combing at the end of the point is especially satisfying for little people since there are mounds of polished rock, sea glass, drift wood and bones at various times of year.

As you walk along the bay side you have a beautiful view of the Inverness Ridge across the way. Look up to your right above the cliffs and you will see a tall pole with a huge stick nest built atop a wooden platform. This is an *osprey's* nest. These birds are raptors (birds of prey with strong talons that hunt animals from the air) with wing spans that reach five feet. Their diet is fish. They nest within sight of their fishing waters. If you visit in the spring, you may be lucky enough to watch the parents returning with fish in their fierce claws to feed their young who are waiting in the nest. Stay quiet and keep your distance so as not to disturb them.

When you reach the tip of the point you must cross a small stream that flows down from the pasture above through the *pickleweed, sea lavender* and *cord grass.* Across the stream is the stretch of pebbly beach that faces the bay. It is strewn with every sort of small treasure from the water: polished stones, water-worn glass, seashells, seaweeds and driftwood.

There is a shallow bog to the right of the parking lot, just beyond the gate where the old ranch road takes off. Here live hundreds of *polliwogs* in various stages of development during the late winter and early spring. Later they develop into *Pacific tree frogs* and *bull frogs* that send up a lively chorus during spring mating season. *Dragon flies* visit the pond on summer days. Later in the season the banks dry up and produce a fragrant cloud of *lavender horsemint* that attracts the local honey bees working to build their stores for the coming winter.

POINT REYES BEACH NORTH and **POINT REYES BEACH SOUTH** are wild and windswept beaches. The beach is quite pitched as a result of the powerful tides that sweep the coastline here - especially during the winter when storms can reform the geography dramatically. You never know what will wash up here from day to day. Parking is right beside the dunes so access is easy. Once down on the beach you can walk for miles in either direction.

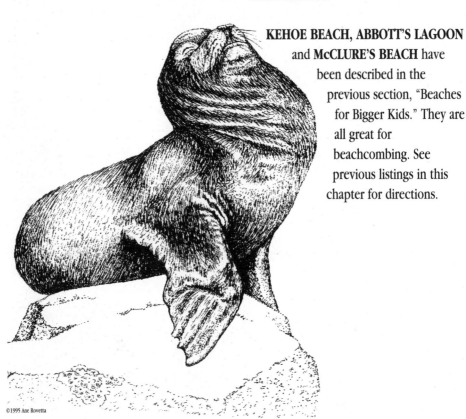

KEHOE BEACH, ABBOTT'S LAGOON and **McCLURE'S BEACH** have been described in the previous section, "Beaches for Bigger Kids." They are all great for beachcombing. See previous listings in this chapter for directions.

©1995 Ane Rovetta

Jellyfish

Story & Illustration by
Ane Rovetta

J ellyfish used to be strong and stout, but he was a hard-headed one. He used to spread any rumor that he heard. He would lie down on the bottom of the ocean, listening to the gossip of the many sea creatures above him, and repeating everything that he heard!

One day he heard a whisper that said, "Fish has stinky socks!" Jellyfish laughed so hard he shook. He decided to go look for those socks. Some animals were whispering.

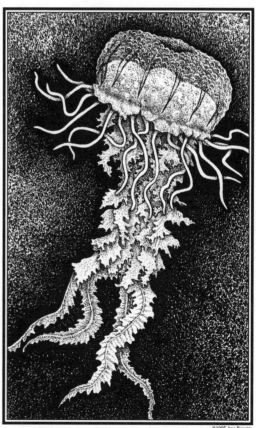

Jellyfish heard one of them say, "Fish hangs his stinky socks from the cliff." So, Jellyfish, he ran out of that ocean, and started up the cliff! He crawled higher and higher, all the time searching for some socks. When he was almost to the top, Jellyfish's feet let go and he fell. It seemed to him he fell through the air forever, but soon he hit the sand. Smeesh! He felt so weak that he couldn't get up! But, the ocean, it knows everything that goes on.

It was the ocean who came to comfort Jellyfish. That water, it asked if Jellyfish was still going to listen to whispers? Was Jellyfish still going to spread mean stories about other animals? Jellyfish promised he wouldn't. "I'll never tease other animals again," he said. So, the ocean, that water got all around the jellyfish, and very gently it rocked him, it lifted him, it picked him up. And they say, the ocean still carries that jellyfish, the sea floats him wherever he wants to go!

FIELD NOTES

FIELD NOTES

Child Hiking Muddy Hollow Trail *California Newt and Nettle Border*
©1995 Karen Gray

Chapter 4

Hit the Trail !
Hiking the Magical Terrain of Point Reyes

The greater Point Reyes area offers you trails in all kinds of environments: sea coast, open meadows, chaparral, dense woodland and pasture lands. All kinds of terrain are here too: gentle walks, switchback trails through the canyons, and trails along the beachside cliffs. It is extraordinary for such a small area to encompass such a richly varied landscape. You can even traverse all of these environments on the same hike in Point Reyes.

The choices and combinations are many. I do not attempt a complete chronicling here of all the hiking trails in the Point Reyes area, only those that I think are especially suited for a particular age or mode of getting around. Truth to tell: every one of the trails in Point Reyes is beautiful and fascinating if you only have your eyes open.

WHEELCHAIR ACCESSIBLE & REST STOP TRAILS

Because Point Reyes is considered a wilderness park, it has been spared many of the so-called "improvements" of more developed parks in the country. However, this sometimes presents difficulties for the elderly or people in wheelchairs, so my first collection of trails will be for them.

As local Garrett Whitt who consulted on this chapter pointed out, there is access and there is access. Some people have operator chairs that are narrow, some have motorized chairs that are wide; some are equipped with all-terrain tires, some not. In this section I provide as much information about the gradient, width and surface of a particular trail as I can. For definitive information regarding wheelchair access, call the Park Service trail maintenance people at (415) 663-8522.

BEAR VALLEY TRAIL

• Water at trailhead only • Restrooms at trailhead and Divide Meadow
• Carry binoculars
• 1.6 Miles to Divide Meadow
• 4.1 Miles to Arch Rock and the ocean

DIRECTIONS: From Point Reyes Station head south on Highway #1. Just over the green bridge take an immediate right onto Sir Francis Drake Boulevard. Take the first left (minding the on-coming traffic from around the blind curve). About a mile down you will see the marked right turn for the Point Reyes National Seashore Headquarters. Follow this drive to the end, past the barn-like Bear Valley Visitor Center. Park in the lot and head out from the main trailhead with the information kiosk. Trailhead about 2 miles from Point Reyes Station.

WARNING: This trail is used by mountain bikers who may not resist the temptation to hurtle down the slope back to the trailhead at high speed. Stay right and listen for approaching bikes behind you.

This trail is my all-time/all-people favorite for nearly any combination of ages and agility. It is the old Bear Valley Road that people traveled by horse-drawn carriage to the hunting lodge that existed in Divide Meadow until the early 1900s. The lodge is now gone, but the knoll on which it sat with the stately *Douglas fir* trees and sweeping view down across the meadow are still there waiting for you.

From the time my son was a newborn in a front-sling pack until now, as a hiking preschooler, we never tire of the changing scene along Bear Valley Trail. For nearly twenty years this has been my first choice for brisk exercise with local friends at any time of day or year. It is the trail I choose when my mother and my aunt, both in their seventies, come to visit. Local joggers use Bear Valley Trail because it starts out nearly level, moves into a gentle incline, and provides a number of natural turn-around spots along the way. The trip back from Divide Meadow is a gentle glide down the slope to the trailhead.

Bear Valley trail is not paved; the surface is somewhat rocky, hard-packed, decomposed granite that is well maintained and very wide. It holds its surface even in very stormy weather (read: "no muddy potholes"). The first stretches of the trail through the Bear Valley meadow parallel the burbling creek. The trail is nearly level for a good third of a mile into the woods. It then begins a gradual climb for another quarter of a mile before it pitches up fairly steeply for the last fifty yards to Divide Meadow, so called because this is where the watershed divides: Coast Creek turns here to run south to the ocean and Bear Valley Creek drains north from here to its outlet at Tomales Bay. The parade of creatures on the trail is always a delight to me: solitary birders with binoculars, hiking groups loaded up with gear piled high for an overnight in one of the campgrounds, people on horseback, wheelchairs, babies in jogger-strollers, joggers, naturalist seminars, deer, cottontails - all of these speaking any number of languages.

As you head out the trail, it cuts through the open meadow where *axis deer, fallow deer* and *black-tailed deer* feed. Brought here in the late 1940s from India, the axis deer are shy and graceful, and produce fawns at any time of the year. They have a reddish brown coat with white spots that are visible throughout the year. A white "bib" on their chest and a dark stripe that runs the length of their back are distinguishing features. The bucks' antlers are shed every winter.

The fallow deer are native to the Mediterranean region of Europe and Asia Minor. They are a source of great delight for visitors because of their color variation: individuals can be black, light brown, chocolate brown, pure white, or spotted. The sight of a pure white deer, looking for all the world like that creature of myth, the unicorn (without the requisite single horn, of course) may be cause for amazed speculation. On closer inspection you'll see that these deer are built as much like goats as deer. Their antlers are palmate, similar to a moose antler. These are not shed until April. Both of these exotic species were introduced for hunting.

The black-tailed or "mule-deer" are our native species and recognizable, as the name tells you, by it's black tail which becomes a white flag when flicked upwards to expose the underside. *Bush rabbits*, or "cottontails," are a frequent sight along the trail as well as pairs of fawns, who all come down the mountainside to drink from Bear Valley Creek.

As the trail gently ascends toward Divide Meadow, it is bordered by an *oak, bay* and *Douglas fir* forest with *alder* trees congregating along the creekside, as they like to stand with their roots near the water. In the spring, Bear Valley Trail is trimmed first in white *milkmaids,* then *blue forget-me-nots, yellow buttercups, maidenhair fern, chain fern,* and *five-fingered fern.* Later in the season, pink *star flower* and *pink flowering currant* appear. This trail offers superb opportunities for close-up study of flora because of the high, vegetated banks on the west-facing side. Originally cut for the old wagon road, the banks have become densely populated with a wide variety of plants and insects at perfect eye level for wheelchairs and children - a vertical garden.

Just about a quarter-mile up the trail keep an eye on the creekbed to your left. You will notice a tall, spindly tree with shaggy red bark. In the fall it will turn a dead-looking rust brown; in the winter it will have no needles; and in the spring and summer it will look very like a redwood tree with bright green needles. This is the famous *dawn redwood,* known only through fossil remains as an extinct species until it was discovered growing halfway up the Yangtze River in the Szechwan Province of China in 1941. Thought to be related to the swamp cypress native to the southern United States, the dawn redwood is a true conifer (supposedly 'evergreen') that loses its needles much as the deciduous broad-leaved trees shed their leaves. Botanists brought back seeds from China and the dawn redwood was celebrated for some time - it was planted in botanical gardens from England to California.

In April you may be lucky enough to spot a magnificent *pacific coast dogwood* in bright bloom in a clearing across the creek to your left. It is a beautiful specimen, very tall and broad, silhouetted against the cliff. Its large, saucer-shaped white blossoms virtually glow in the sunshine. When the tree is in full bloom it looks like it is covered in little white doves perched on the branches for a rest.

Both of these trees were planted by the owner of an old summer cabin, Robert Menzies, an early California botanist after whom a number of our native species are named. The summer cabin is gone, and a field of *stinging nettles* hold sway through most of the spring and summer, so you would be wise to satisfy yourself with admiring the dogwood from the trail.

It was just around here one spring that my Mother and I, on the way back from a hike, noticed something hanging in pendulous masses from the branches along the cliffside: thousands of *lady bugs,* all but invisible against the reddish brown of dead leaves and bark on the bank. They must have been camouflaged in the cold of early morning as we headed up, but now they were moving in the full rays of warm sunshine just creeping into the valley. There are several species of lady bug. The one that gathers here in winter and spring tend to congregate in large clusters in order to share warmth.

All along Bear Valley Trail there are sections of gargantuan logs cut roughly to provide benches for resting. These are great fun for children because of their scale. They look like custom-built giant's furniture in the woods. Their addition also makes Bear Valley a good trail for those who like to walk but need places to rest along the way. You can, of course, turn around at any point.

If you do reach Divide Meadow there are more log seats, a picnic table and a lovely mowed bench of grass beneath giant *Douglas firs.* If you visit in late August you will be treated to the unlikely sight of a double chorus line of pink "naked ladies " at the far end of the meadow, shining and shocking in the sun. These are old world *amaryllis lilies,* probably planted by the owners of the hunting lodge many years ago. Because they are not palatable to gophers or other wildlife and because their large bulbs hold water and nutrients through the long California dry season, these lilies will survive with no cultivation at all for decades, long after their caretakers have gone. They are often all that remains of nineteenth century farms or old cemeteries. Traveling up the coast of California in August, when all around is weathered fenceposts and golden grass, you will glimpse a stand of these exotic pink flowers floating alone above the ground on red stems without benefit of greenery, and know that once a family lived there or maybe someone was buried there. Amaryllis are sweetly fragrant, making this spot in Divide Meadow a wonderful place to lie down for a rest before continuing on.

From Divide Meadow the trail dips down a slope to the marshy area below, then continues out at a very gradual slope through the dappled shade of alder trees and along the streamside to the ocean. For the entire length of your walk, you will have the company of the burbling creek.

EARTHQUAKE TRAIL

• Water fountain • Wheelchair accessible • Restrooms • Picnic tables
• Good site for drawing and painting • 0.6 mile loop

DIRECTIONS: Head south on Highway #1 from Point Reyes Station. Take an immediate right after the green bridge. Follow Sir Francis Drake Boulevard to the first left onto Bear Valley Road (watch for on-coming traffic around the blind curve). Take a right at the sign for the Point Reyes National Seashore Headquarters and Bear Valley Visitor Center. Park at the end of the road in the large lot on the left. The Earthquake Trail takes off behind the restroom building. Trailhead about 2 miles from Point Reyes Station.

The Earthquake Trail has interpretive stations to orient the visitor to the surrounding geology, landscape and, of course, the *San Andreas Fault Line* - famous for the 1906 earthquake that shook San Francisco. The trail leads through the grassland toward Bear Valley Creek. It parallels the creek for some distance then crosses again and heads back to the picnic area. In the spring the wildflowers are beautiful. The canopy of *oak* and *bay* has a wonderful fragrance in the cooler months after a rain. Varieties of *mushrooms* can be spotted here in the warm, rainy months. *Deer* often browse in the meadow, which is a great place for flying kites.

This trail is a good one to combine with a trip to the Bear Valley Visitor Center across the road, and a picnic in the *Douglas fir* grove. Here you can watch the colony of *acorn woodpeckers* work at storing acorns in the bark of the trees as they hop up and down the trunks with their red heads bobbing.

JOHNSTONE-JEPSON TRAIL LOOP

• Carry water • No restrooms • Carry binoculars
• Good views across Tomales Bay from rest stop • 3.0 mile loop

DIRECTIONS: From the town of Point Reyes Station head south on Highway #1. Take an immediate right onto Sir Francis Drake Boulevard after the green bridge. Follow Sir Francis Drake through Inverness and over the hill. Bear right at the "Y" onto Pierce Point Ranch Road. Watch for the sign for the Johnstone Trail and small parking area on the right. Trailhead about 10 miles from Point Reyes Station.

This last trail is steep. It is distinguished by a series of thoughtfully placed clearings with benches in the woods that offer lovely views of Tomales Bay and the hills beyond.

Follow the Jepson Trail through the woods leading down half a mile to the Jepson Memorial Grove. The grove is a stand of the ancient *bishop pine*, stately and gnarled. The undergrowth in these woods is especially varied and interesting: *salal, huckleberry, sword fern, blue elderberry, chain ferns, sea foam, pink flowering currant, wild gooseberry, hazelnut, toyon, coffeeberry, wild ginger, indian cucumber* and, of course, *poison oak. Mushrooms* pop up everywhere during the warm rainy months. The trail is a switchback that is good for pacing yourself and not too steep.

A half-mile past the grove, the trail comes to Heart's Desire Beach. You can go back up the trail the way you came from your car, or you can walk south down the beach and pick up the Johnstone Trail. Just a short ways up on a promontory overlooking the bay is a small picnic area with barbecues under the oaks. Continuing on, the trail winds up through the woods and back to the trailhead at Sir Francis Drake Boulevard.

ABBOTT'S LAGOON TRAIL TO THE FOOTBRIDGE

• Restrooms at Trailhead • Carry Water
1.5 Miles to Lagoon

DIRECTIONS: From the town of Point Reyes Station take Highway #1 south over the green bridge. Make an immediate right onto Sir Francis Drake Boulevard. Follow Sir Francis Drake through Inverness and up the hill. Bear right at the "Y" in the road onto Pierce Point Ranch Road. Follow it out through the ranch lands to the marked trailhead for Abbott's Lagoon on the left. Trailhead about 10 mile from Point Reyes Station.

This trail follows a meandering route through gently sloping pasturelands to the lagoon. The trail is hard-packed dirt maintained by the park for wheelchair access. Blue and yellow *bush lupine* predominate on the hillsides, providing habitat for song birds and hunting grounds for raptors: *red-tailed hawks, golden eagles, northern harriers* (marsh hawks), *kestrels* and *owls*.

This is a particularly beautiful trail because of the blending of open grassland and chaparral combined with the water courses and lagoon. In the springtime when the yellow bush lupine is in bloom its spicy fragrance is intoxicating.

PIERCE POINT RANCH SELF-GUIDED TOUR

• Carry water • Picnic Table • Restrooms at McClure's Beach trailhead
• Good site for drawing and painting • Walk is adjacent to parking area

DIRECTIONS: Take Highway #1 south from Point Reyes Station. Just over the green bridge make an immediate right onto Sir Francis Drake Boulevard. Follow this road through the town of Inverness and over the ridge. Bear right onto Pierce Point Ranch Road when the road forks. Follow this all the way out to the end, parking in the small lot in front of the compound of white-washed buildings. Trailhead about 22 miles from Point Reyes Station.

Pierce Point Ranch is about a thirty-minute drive from town - and what a beautiful drive it is, skirting the ancient *bishop pines* and revealing an expansive view of the Pacific ocean as you crest the ridge. The road then winds through miles of rolling ranch lands high enough to provide views of the mountain ranges to the north, east and south.

The old ranch buildings have been preserved in their 19th century, white-washed simplicity. The entire site is a level grassland on hard-packed dirt. An excellent collection of interpretive stations at each building explains with words and drawings what life was like for the adults and children who lived out in this remote place. The cow barn is restored and open (a ramp leads into the open door on the north side).

I recently visited this place with my husband and son, on a warm fall day with the ocean mists blowing in opaque drifts across the brown hills. We sat at the picnic table beside the cow barn in the yard, sheltered from wind, listening to the big, black ravens in the old *cypress* trees raucously calling to each other. Across the saddle in the hills to the south, a harem of *tule elk* grazed and lounged in the chaparral. There was a *red tailed hawk* high up in the *eucalyptus* trees beyond the ranch house calling as it swooped down across the open grassland. My son was enchanted with the place - as much for the plethora of golden grasshoppers he could chase and catch as with the dark, mysterious barn standing empty of cows but obviously hosting other creatures (barn owls? bats? field mice? wood rats? ghosts?).

ESTERO TRAIL

• Restrooms • Carry water • Carry binoculars • 2.5 miles each way

DIRECTIONS: From the town of Point Reyes Station head south on Highway #1. Take an immediate right onto Sir Francis Drake Boulevard after the green bridge. Follow Sir Francis Drake through Inverness and over the hill bearing left where the road splits. You will see the sign for Estero Trail just past the turn-off for Mt. Vision. Trailhead about 10 miles from Point Reyes Station.

Estero Trail has been designed for wheelchair access. The trail is a gentle grade of crushed rock that meanders through open pasture lands. This is one of the most beautiful spots for seeing wild *Douglas iris* in the late winter and early spring. The plants form large masses in the grass (neatly clipped into lawn by the grazing cows) that vary in their shades of deep purple, lavender, mauve, gold and cream.

After about a half-mile, the trail winds through a *pine* wood, a former Christmas tree farm, where *owls* roost during the day. Coming through the wood you will get your first glimpse of Home Bay and Drake's Estero. Where the wooden bridge crosses the estero we have seen young *bat rays* fluttering together in the shallow water under the bridge, dark brown and mysterious, holding their place with precision as the fresh water rushed out with the receding tide.

Here to the right, around the shoreline, is a little rocky beach with a grassy bluff above. Depending on the tide, either place can be hospitable for a rest and picnic before heading back.

WARNING: Harbor seals haul out here to rest and have their pups. Do not approach them. They are very vulnerable to disturbance. Should you see an animal that you think is in distress call the Marine Mammal Center at (415) 289-7325.

CROSS MARIN TRAIL

• No restrooms • Carry water • Paved surface
• 3.0 miles one way (minimal gradient)

DIRECTIONS: From the town of Point Reyes Station head south on Highway #1 for 2 miles. At the flashing stoplight in Olema take a left onto Sir Francis Drake Boulevard heading east. Go up and over Olema hill. In about 2 miles you will see the sign for the Cross Marin Trailhead. Turn left following the marker and park on the roadside. The trail begins here, leading underneath Sir Francis Drake Boulevard and into the redwood trees. Trailhead about 4 miles from Point Reyes Station.

This trail follows beautiful Lagunitas Creek for some miles along the old railroad grade and finally comes out at the Irving Camp and group picnic area in Samuel P. Taylor State Park. The path winds under stately *coast redwood* trees, past an old ranch site with gnarled *apple* trees and a *eucalyptus* grove, then out into an open meadow that is strewn with wildflowers in the spring. In a few places there is easy shallow access down to the creekside for children to wade in the water and study the wildlife on the banks. *Big leaf maple*, never far from a streamside, turn a brilliant gold in fall and dangle long, elegant pink catkins in the early spring. Their leaves float downstream like small yellow boats on the water with the first autumn winds. *Great blue herons* can be seen fishing stealthily here. *Deer* are common. Spawning *coho salmon* can be seen in the riffles of the creek after the first heavy rains (call the ranger station for information 488-9897). ***WARNING: The Cross Marin Trail is an asphalt road that is striped for bicycle traffic***

©1995 Ane Rovetta

in both directions. It's a favorite with cyclists who ride in fast-moving groups, especially on weekends. Be aware of on-coming traffic and keep right.

FIVE BROOK STABLES & AROUND THE OLD MILL POND

• Porta Potties • Washing spigot (not potable) • Carry water • Picnic tables
• Carry binoculars for birding • Good site for drawing and painting
• 0.25 mile walk

DIRECTIONS: Take Highway #1 south from Point Reyes Station. Pass through the hamlet of Olema and over a couple of little bridges. The turn-off for Five Brooks Stables is on the right. The drive leads in toward the stables and then forks. Follow the signs up to the right to the parking lot. From this small plateau above the stables there is a level path leading west to the Old Mill Pond and around its edge. This is the beginning of the Stewart Trail up the ridge, much used by horses. Trailhead about 6 miles from Point Reyes Station.

The trail is well maintained and there are clear spots around the banks of the pond for sitting quietly and watching the bird life. You may see lots of waterfowl, *herons* and *snowy egrets* fishing, *red-winged blackbirds* in the tules, and songbirds in the thickets around the banks. There are a couple of picnic tables strategically placed under the willows for good views. The surrounding hills with their majestic *Douglas fir* and pine forests are beautiful. In the spring there may be foals down below in the stables.

STINSON BEACH PARK

• Restrooms • Running water and fountain • Showers • Barbecues
• Picnic tables • Village adjacent

(This is not really a specific hike, although there is plenty of room for walking and exercising)

DIRECTIONS: Head south on Highway #1 from the town of Point Reyes Station. In about 13 miles you will bear left around Bolinas lagoon, keeping to Highway #1. In about 2 miles you will come into the village of Stinson Beach. The entrance to Stinson Beach Park is clearly marked on the right. Pass the ranger's kiosk and turn left to the picnic grounds parking. About 15 miles south of Point Reyes Station.

This park can be mobbed in the summer months with the cars of city-dwellers backed up all the way through the village and up the side of Mt. Tamalpais. On a beautiful fall or early spring weekday, however, the whole village will be quiet and peaceful. The picnic grounds are a lovely place to share family time.

The tables and barbecues are spaced wide apart so children can play ball and other games. *Willows* and *pine* trees provide dappled shade. The broad path to the beach is paved in asphalt for wheelchair access to the top of the dunes and a view of the ocean.

If you don't want to be bothered packing a picnic, just a short distance across the footbridge and over the creek, there is a restaurant with good fast food, the Parkside Café, where you can get burgers and other things to-go.

The little market in town also specializes in picnic fare.

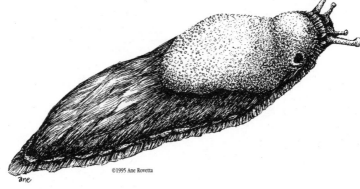

©1995 Ane Rovetta

ane

FIELD NOTES

HIKES WITH CHILDREN IN JOGGER-STROLLERS

Certainly all the trails described in the previous section for wheelchair access are ideal, easy trails for jogger-strollers. (The Jepson/Johnstone Loop is manageable if you are hardy; just be forewarned that it includes steep switchbacks up and down the ridge.) The small wheeled jogger-strollers with mountain-bike tires are great for Point Reyes. We have one with a wire basket on the back for gear, a sunshade for sun or rain, and a locking hand brake for parking on slopes. It collapses flat with just two cotter pins and stores on the roof racks of the car. You can find them used in baby supply stores, or check your local classifieds.

For a child who has outgrown a back pack (or outgrown your back) a jogger-stroller is the perfect link between being carried and learning to hike on her own two feet. She can hike out as far as she is able, then jump in the chariot for a ride and a nap. In this way you can hike for many miles at an adult pace while your child comes along in comfort. You can push the stroller out empty on the first leg of your hike (or carrying your picnic) and then add your child when she is worn out.

My son did go through an exasperating time when he wanted to push his stuffed bear in the stroller along the trail, not ride himself, but, mercifully, it only lasted a few weeks. He couldn't see over the stroller - it was much taller than he was - so he would push headlong off the trail and down the creek bank, landing in a heap of frustration. Fortunately, he outgrew this passion. Now he wants to hike as far as he can and concedes to ride only when he is too tired to go on.

©1995 Ane Rovetta

MARTINELLI'S RANCH TOMALES BAY TRAIL

• No restrooms • Carry water • Carry binoculars
• 2/3 mile to U.S.G.S. marker at viewpoint

DIRECTIONS: Trailhead is about 3 miles north of Point Reyes Station on Highway #1. The turnout for Tomales Bay Trail is clearly marked on the left.

The old Martinelli Ranch is still host to some cattle but they are used to having people in their pasture. Once through the stile, the trail takes off over gently rolling grasslands with a view of the Inverness Ridge ahead. At the fork in the trail, head down to the left towards the old pond. *Ducks, gulls, scoters, herons, geese,* and *swans* all stop over here at different times of year.

The trail crosses over the pond's outlet to Tomales Bay and you can see the village of Inverness across the way. As you climb the steep hill you will come out onto an open plateau that ends in a remarkable view of the bay. With the Inverness Ridge so close and the bay stretched out below you, long and narrow, you see clearly that this is where the Continental plate grinds against the Pacific Plate forming the *San Andreas Faultline.*

The trail turns to the right and crests the hill, then begins to drop down past a large *Douglas fir* tree and disappears into a thicket. It is possible to continue on through the thicket and come out down below on the old railroad trestle that carried the train across the water from Point Reyes Station to Tomales at the turn of the century. Be wary, however: *poison oak* is rampant here.

The view of the bay marsh and pasture below is very good, especially if you brought your binoculars along for spotting birds. Sound carries clearly up from the lively marsh below so if you sit quietly and listen for a while you may hear a good many more animals than you can see.

TOMALES POINT TRAIL

- Nearest restrooms are down the road at McClure's Beach trailhead
- Great site for drawing and painting • Carry Water
- About 4 miles to the end of the trail at the point

DIRECTIONS: Head south on Highway #1. Take an immediate right onto Sir Francis Drake Boulevard after crossing the green bridge. Bear right at the "Y" and proceed through Inverness, up and over the hill. Bear right onto Pierce Point Ranch Road at the next fork in the road. Follow this to the end where you will see the parking area in front of the ranch compound of white-washed buildings. Trailhead is about 22 miles from Point Reyes Station (35 minute drive) .

Park in the area just in front of the ranch. The compound is level and accessible for strollers should you want to tour the grounds and get a feel for what it was like to grow up on such an isolated ranch a century ago. Children here were so far from town they even had their own schoolhouse on the ranch. You can see it, along with the restored milking barn and other buildings, clustered together above the bay. There are good illustrations with explanations of the ranch life in stations around the grounds for a self-guided tour.

The Tomales Point Trail takes off from the parking area under the *cypress* trees and winds behind the old barn to the north. It is a very good trail for jogger-strollers. There are a few places where ruts have developed on steep pitches in the trial, but you can easily maneuver around these, even when the ground is wet. The trail is fairly level for about a mile, and early on you can see the isolated beaches and rolling sea beneath you on your left. Walk along the western slopes of the point until you come to a saddle in the hills where you see historic White's Gulch and Tomales Bay down below you to the east. There is a foot trail here, too narrow for strollers, that leads down to the marsh at the base of the inlet. This is especially good for spotting wildlife (*elk, deer, bobcat*) since they come down to the fresh water in the swale to drink.

After this point the trail begins to dip and climb and you are atop the spine of Tomales Point as it gradually narrows, with a panoramic view of the bay to the east and the Pacific Ocean to the west. This is a perfect platform from which to watch the *gray whales* in their migration. You are high, at eye level with the *turkey vultures* and raptors floating on the thermals that rise up from the beach, with a clear view to the horizon. When you've hiked as far as you can, the only way back is the way you came. The trail goes another .8 miles or so to Tomales Point.

ESTERO TRAIL - BEYOND THE BRIDGE

• Carry water • Restrooms at trailhead • Carry binoculars
• 2 1/2 miles one way

DIRECTIONS: From the town of Point Reyes Station head south on Highway #1. Take an immediate right onto Sir Francis Drake Boulevard after crossing the green bridge. Proceed on through Inverness and up and over the ridge. Bear left at the "Y", keeping to Sir Francis Drake Blvd. The turn-off for Estero Trail is marked on the left side of the road, just beyond the road for Mt. Vision. Go down the ranch road about 1 mile where you will see the trailhead on the right. About 10 miles from Point Reyes Station. (For a description of the trail from the trailhead to the estero check the previous section "Estero Trail to the Footbridge.")

When you cross the bridge you will see a pond on the far side over the inlet with *tules* growing and a good population of *bull frogs* and *tree frogs* that you will be more likely to hear than to see. *Ducks, herons, dragonflies, butterflies* and *salamanders* can all be found here in season. There are a couple of easy places to get down to the water's edge to observe the *water skaters* and other residents of the pond community.

You can forge ahead up the steep trail cut into the far hillside and hike around the bend. The visible steep stretch, however, is devilish clay that turns to gummy, slick goo after a rain and foils the most intrepid hikers. We are still scraping the mud off the stroller tires from the last time we tried to slip and slide over this patch.

Once around the bend, you unlatch the wire gate (being sure to put it back) and level out on an old ranch road that skirts the western slopes high above Drake's Estero. You get a good view of Johnson's *oyster beds* (all those sticks poking out of the water at low tide) and the waterfowl that stop here. *Harbor seals* come into the estero for rest so keep your eyes peeled for a jumble of silver gray, weathered logs that move on the opposite shore.

There are clearings in the brambles along the bluff edge for sitting, but beware:

poison oak is here looking like *blackberry* vine. The trail dips and climbs heading west towards the sea and along the estero. About a half-mile beyond the bridge you come to an old, wind-torn *eucalyptus* tree that was part of the dairy ranch here years ago. This is a lovely promontory for a rest and a picnic. Islands of *Douglas iris* are everywhere.

Nearly two and a half miles from the bridge, there is a fork in the trail; the Estero Trail goes left to Limantour Estero and the Sunset Beach Trail continues out towards the ocean another mile and a half. It climbs up to two freshwater ponds at the point, with beautiful views of Drake's Estero and the Pacific. You must return by the same route.

LIMANTOUR ESTERO TRAIL

• Water faucet at the trailhead • Restrooms at trailhead
• Carry binoculars and hand lens • 0.25 mile loop

DIRECTIONS: From Point Reyes Station, head south on Highway #1. Just over the green bridge take an immediate right onto Sir Francis Drake Boulevard. Turn left at the "Y" onto Bear Valley Road (watch for on-coming traffic around the blind curve). Just a quarter mile down take a right at the sign for Limantour Beach. Follow Limantour Road to the end and park (about 5 miles). The trailhead is just below the restrooms. Trailhead about 6 miles from Point Reyes Station.

From the parking lot, go around the cattle gate on the south side of the trailhead. You will come out on the asphalt paved path that crosses over the estero. The trail along the edge of the estero takes off on the far side to the right. It eventually just dies out in the dunes about three-quarters of the way down. The trail is not pruned or paved regularly so it is best to visit in dry weather to avoid muddy potholes. It can be narrow with overhanging *bush lupine* and *baccharis* (commonly called 'coyote brush') but is usually passable.

The estero provides wonderful opportunities to view waterfowl, raptors, *great blue herons* and *snowy egrets* that fish here. The broad trail is bordered by a baccharis and *blackberry* thicket, but is kept low in places so you can get good views of the water from chair level. The thicket hosts many wrens and songbirds at various times of year.

NOTE: Limantour Beach is accessible by wheelchair along the asphalt road to the top of the dunes and a view of the ocean.

UPDATE: This area burned through in the Mt. Vision fire of October 1995. Watch for dramatic changes in vegetation - will the alder trees rejuvenate?

MUDDY HOLLOW TRAIL

• Carry water • Nearest restrooms are down the road 1 mile at Limantour Beach

(Note: there's no place to stop and rest along the trail before you reach the
end because of stinging nettle and poison oak.)

**DIRECTIONS: From the town of Point Reyes Station head south on Highway #1.
Immediately after the green bridge turn right onto Sir Francis Drake Boulevard.
When the road forks, turn left onto Bear Valley Road (being mindful of oncoming
traffic around the blind curve). The second right is Limantour Road.**

The trail takes off level through *alder* trees and dappled sunlight. This is a good
trail most any time of year since it is shielded from winds, and open to sunshine. The trail
follows a creek all the way to the sand dunes at Limantour Beach. Muddy Hollow is
bordered by dense thickets of *blackberry, salmonberry,
ollalie berry* and *baccharis.* Beware, however, *poison oak* is
hiding in there, too. These thickets are home to any number
of songbirds that nest and feed in them. If you stop and listen
you may not see them but you will hear their songs. This trail
is also cursed with a dense edging of *stinging nettle* that
thrives in the boggy soil from spring clear through the
summer. Wear long sleeves, long pants and be wary.

Keep a lookout for
large mounds of piled-up sticks
along the banks of the pond.
These are home to the
muskrats who build their multi-
storied homes of mud and *tules*
where they make bedrooms for
sleeping, nurseries for their young, and
pantries for storing their food. Muskrats always
live at the water's edge - either freshwater pond
or stream bank. They may be seen (if you are
very quiet) gliding across the surface of the

©1995 Ane Rovetta

pond on a foray.

(There is a wonderful muskrat house, carefully cut in half for viewing the inside rooms, in the California wing of the Oakland Museum. It looks for all the world like a dollhouse - the ones made in open style with the various floors visible so you can change the furniture easily. All the rooms are there, furnished a little differently than a human house, yes, but furnished just the same with sticks, mud, thistle down, bottle caps, tin foil, cattail down, leaves, gum wrappers and other essentials.)

As he sat on the grass and looked across the river, a dark hole in the bank opposite, just above the water's edge, caught his eye, and dreamily he fell to considering what a nice snug dwelling-place it would make for an animal with few wants and fond of a bijou riverside residence, above flood level and remote from noise and dust. As he gazed, something bright and small seemed to twinkle down in the heart of it, vanished, then twinkled once more like a tiny star. But it could hardly be a star in such an unlikely situation, and it was too glittering and small for a glow-worm. Then, as he looked, it winked at him, and so declared itself to be an eye; and a small face began gradually to grow up round it, like a frame round a picture.

A brown little face, with whiskers.

A grave round face, with the same twinkle in its eye that had first attracted his notice.

Small neat ears and thick silky hair. It was the Water Rat!

–from Wind in the Willows *by Kenneth Grahame*

Another lover of bogs that you will see here in spring is the poison *hemlock,* killer of the famous philosopher Socrates in ancient Greece, who was made to drink a potion of the stuff for his radical teaching. It is one of the many "wayside weeds" brought here from the old world with the settlers years ago. It has a lacy, light-green leaf with many umbells of delicate white flowers held on tall branching stalks that are mottled with brown. I have a wildflower and wayside weeds field guide from England that describes hemlock as smelling "like wet mouse fur." I thought that this description was ridiculous - after all, how many of us have ever had the opportunity to get a whiff of a wet mouse? - until I was removing a patch of hemlock from my garden and I found that it does, indeed, smell like wet mouse fur! How do I know? Instinctive memory? That's another mystery of Mother Nature, I guess. See what you think. (Wash your hands afterwards).

The pond is just about 1.2 miles up the trail. Go another 0.6 miles and you will come out behind the parking lot for Limantour Beach. This will bring you back to the end of Limantour Road and a very steep hike up the road to the Muddy Hollow turn-off, about 1/4 mile; or you can go back the way you came.

WARNING: The last stretch of this trail gets predictably muddy and unpleasant during the rainy season. A dense layer of clay between the pond and the estero can make for a ruined pair of boots and very slick going (gooing?).

©1995 Ane Rovetta

COAST TRAIL TO BASS LAKE & ALAMERE FALLS

• Carry water • Carry binoculars • Porta-potties at trailhead (100 yards down the trail in the eucalyptus grove) • 8.0 miles round trip

DIRECTIONS: Head south on Highway #1 from the town of Point Reyes Station. In about 12 miles Highway #1 forms a junction with the Olema-Bolinas Road. Bear right towards Bolinas and follow the road along the Bolinas Lagoon to the stop sign. Turn left at the sign (this keeps you on the Olema-Bolinas Road) and proceed to the next stop sign. Take a right onto Mesa Road and follow it out to the end (about 6 miles) and park in the trailhead lot. Trailhead about 22 miles from Point Reyes Station.

Parts of the Coast Trail seem suspended high over the ocean in the same way as trails do on the Big Sur Coast: you are up among the birds with a clear view way out to the Farallon Islands on the horizon. The spring wildflowers here are profuse.

The trail takes you through a *eucalyptus* grove and out onto the southern tip of the Point Reyes National Seashore. It skirts wooded canyons and ravines for a couple of miles, dipping down and climbing back up again many times. Creeks from inland lakes rush down to the ocean here and create hospitable places for flora and fauna to thrive. The cover is good for wild animals and the fresh water supports a wide variety of trees and plants.

After 1.2 miles along the cliff edge the trail turns in for another 1.5 miles until you reach Bass Lake, edged in *tules* and hosting a variety of water birds around its rim, depending on the season. This is a favorite lake for local swimming during warm summer days. (Swim at your own risk.) It can be good for birdwatching in the colder months.

If you continue another three-quarters of a mile through open grassland you will come to Alamere Falls. In the winter and early spring, after heavy rains, the falls offer a wonderful sound as well as sight as the water crashes down the cliff to the beach far below.

FIELD NOTES

WALKS FOR PRESCHOOLERS

Flora and fauna at eye level and water - in any form - define a great hike for my son. At nearly four he is just beginning to use his screened bug house for creature study and the wildlife guides for species identification (I read, he uses the illustrations). Streamsides, ponds, waterfalls at the beach, are all cause for jubilation with preschoolers. The collection of forays below offers a good variety of environments for all kinds of weather.

MILLERTON POINT STATE PARK

• Restroom at trailhead • Carry water • Barbecue and Picnic Table across the footbridge
• 1.0 mile loop along the bluff • 1.0 mile loop along the beach

DIRECTIONS: Trailhead about 3 miles north of Point Reyes Station on Highway #1. The clearly marked turn-off is on the left.

This was an old ranch so you'll see the *eucalyptus* grove and an old barn. A clearly visible *osprey's* nest, small pond in winter and spring (land-locked, so count on it only after some good rains), and a delightful little beach filled with waterborne treasures are all here.

An easy, level hike loops through the grassland. It takes off just through the metal gate on the right by the parking area. Wear your boots in rainy weather; there are some marshy patches. Because this promontory is no longer grazed, the grass is high and wildflowers are wonderful here in spring. You have great views of the bay and Inverness Ridge. When you get around to the north where the trail skirts the cliff edge, you can see the *oyster beds* of the commercial oyster growers in the bay (rows of vertical sticks that are exposed above the water).

This beach is a good choice for cold and blustery days because it faces south and the bluffs protect it from the prevailing winds.

BEAR VALLEY TRAIL

- Restrooms at Trailhead and Divide Meadow • Carry water
- 3.2 miles round trip to Divide Meadow
- 8.2 miles round trip to Arch Rock and the ocean. Resting benches along the way

DIRECTIONS: From the town of Point Reyes Station head south on Highway #1. Just over the green bridge, turn right onto Sir Francis Drake Boulevard. In about a mile the road will split at the base of Inverness Ridge. Bear left onto Bear Valley Road . (Beware of on-coming traffic around the blind curve!) Proceed for about a mile to the main entrance to the Point Reyes Natioinal Seashore on your right. Follow the drive to the end and park. The trailhead is at the main gate beside the information kiosk. Trailhead about 2 miles from Point Reyes Station.

Bear Valley is a superb trail for little people: it's nearly level for quite a stretch, it borders the creek, and there is a rich array of flora on the cliff bank at lower levels. This trail is great on hot days because of the dappled sunlight, and on rainy days because the forest canopy offers quite a bit of shelter. I do not recommend it for really cold days in winter - sometimes the frost never melts and the damp can be bone-chilling.

Access to the creek is very easy in a couple of spots where the trail dips down nearer the water. Be careful not to scramble down the steep banks to the water, as this erodes the dirt banks and destroys the plant cover that helps control erosion. Once down at streamside you can lift any rock in the creek and find the nymphs of *caddis flies* or *May flies* covered in granular camouflage attached to the underside of the rocks. Small fish, *tree frogs, salamanders* and *snakes* may all be found for study.

NOTE: See the beginning of this chapter - "Bear Valley: The All-persons/All-time Favorite"- for a full description.

WOODPECKER TRAIL

• Water and restrooms at Visitor Center • Carry binoculars • 0.7 Mile loop

DIRECTIONS: Follow the directions for Bear Valley Trail above. Trailhead about 2 miles from Point Reyes Station.

A natural adjunct to your time at the Bear Valley Visitor Center is a walk around the Woodpecker Trail. This is a self-guided tour; informative trailside plaques along the way explain what you see. A nearly level loop, the trail takes off on the right just inside the trailhead for Bear Valley Trail. You walk up the hill through the grass and past the Morgan Horse Ranch. Soon you enter the dense *bay, Douglas fir* and *oak* woods.

Stop for a moment an listen carefully. You may hear the raucous yelling and chatter of the *acorn woodpeckers* up in the canopy ("Jacob! Jacob! Jacob!") As they bob up and down in their storage trees ("granaries"), stocking their pantries, you can see their bright red heads and black and white bodies. When they swoop from tree to tree you will see flashes of black-and-white stripes. If you see flashes of dark brown and white with bright orange under the wings, you have spotted a *red-shafted flicker*, a woodpecker family member and also a resident of this wood.

About half a mile through the forest a footbridge crosses Sky Creek and the plant life is dense: *ferns, huckleberry, coffee berry, wild lilac*. Many birds and small mammals make their homes here, so be on the lookout.

The trail loops around, re-crosses the creek and takes you back to the Bear Valley parking area. This is a good trail for nearly any weather: wildflowers in the spring, mushrooms in the winter and lots of animals.

KULE LOKLO INDIAN VILLAGE
& AROUND THE MORGAN HORSE RANCH

• Water fountain outside Tack Room at Ranch and at storage shed at Kule Loklo Indian
Village • Porta Potty at Ranch • 1.0 mile loop

**DIRECTIONS: Follow the directions for Bear Valley Trail above. All amenities are at
the Bear Valley Visitor Center.**

This walk is another natural with children after you have toured the Bear Valley
Visitor Center. Begin at the north end of the horse pasture behind the center. Climb
gradually up the hill with *oak* woods on your right and the pasture on your left, for an
eighth of a mile. At the *eucalyptus* grove turn in on the right and walk through the trees.

Soon you come out in a level clearing that holds a recreated village of traditional
Coast Miwok Indian structures. This spot commands a beautiful view of the mountains to
the east: Elephant Mountain, Bolinas Ridge and Mt. Barnaby. If you go back through the
eucalyptus trees you can take the same trail, as it continues around the Morgan horse
pasture in a big loop, ending at the Morgan Horse Ranch and back down at the parking lot.
Along the way, you will wind through dense forest with large *bay t*rees and mysterious old
hollow stumps (who lives in there??) You will skirt the uphill side of the pasture where
horses are often grazing nearby. In the spring there may be foals here.

RANDALL TRAIL & HAGMAIER'S POND

• No Restrooms • Carry water • 1.5 mile loop

DIRECTIONS: South of Point Reyes Station on Highway #1 (before the hamlet of Dogtown) is a large pullout on the right and a sign marking the Randall Trail on the left side of the road just at the cattle gate. Trailhead about 8 miles south of Point Reyes Station.

To reach the pond you will enter a *Douglas fir* and *oak* woods that is a special delight on misty, rainy days. *Ferns, mushrooms, wild ginger, huckleberry* and *salal* carpet the ground.

Follow the trail that takes off on the right just beyond the cattle gate and you will come up to two large ponds created years ago by damming the creek for cattle. These are popular ponds for swimming in the summertime. My favorite time to visit them, though, is winter. In the late winter and early spring the ponds are the destination of the *California newts* that travel long distances through the woods to congregate in the shallows for mating.

Last spring, on a heavily misting day, we set out with my son and a little friend in our galoshes and raincoats in search of the newts. We slogged all around the ponds, finding and studying *polliwogs* in all phases, but no newts. We decided to hike up the steep ridge into the woods for some exercise and there - slowly waggling across the dirt fire road - was a beautiful newt: glossy, rubbery brown with a bright orange underside. Its eyes were quite expressive. The newt was wonderful for my son to hold and study because he was slow-moving and not easily injured. As we replaced it on the trail, it knowingly re-positioned itself in the same direction as it was headed before and continued on its way.

Randall Trail pitches nearly straight up the ridge to its junction with the Bolinas Ridge Trail at the top. It is a steep climb and you may turn around at any point to go back down. It is about 2 miles from Highway #1 up to Bolinas Ridge.

FIELD NOTES

HIKES FOR OLDER CHILDREN

FERN CANYON TRAIL

• Carry water • Restrooms at Point Reyes Bird Observatory • 2.0 mile loop

DIRECTIONS: Head south on Highway #1 from the town of Point Reyes Station. In about 12 miles Highway #1 forms a junction with the Olema-Bolinas Road. Bear right towards Bolinas and follow the road along the Bolinas Lagoon to the stop sign. Turn left at the sign (this keeps you on the Olema-Bolinas Road) and proceed to the next stop sign. Take a right onto Mesa Road and follow it out to the PRBO field station (about 6 miles) and park in the lot. Trailhead about 22 miles from Point Reyes Station.

Fern Canyon Trail is the perfect adjunct to your visit to the Point Reyes Bird Observatory. The staff there will provide you with an illustrated booklet ("Fern Canyon Guide") that makes this trail self-guiding.

At the east side of the parking area for PRBO you take off through chaparral and grassland. About a quarter-mile in, you come to a lookout on the bluff where you can see the deep green canyon down below. Just beyond the overlook the trail descends steeply into Fern Canyon and you will see that it is aptly named. The dense canopy of trees above provides the perfect shade for the streambanks to host a variety of lush ferns: *western sword ferns, lady fingers, polypody ferns,* and *five-fingered ferns* all thrive here.

About a half-mile from the trailhead you climb down a wooden ladder into a little glen. This is a lovely spot for a picnic and some study of the surrounding flora. When you start out again, cross the footbridge over the creek and climb the steep steps up the canyonside. You will pass through a group of imposing old *buckeye* trees, then on to Miwok Meadows, the site of an old Coast Miwok Indian camp. Past the meadow you will come out of the canyon and back through the coastal chaparral. The trail arrives at Mesa Road three-quarters of a mile up from the parking area. Turn left onto the road and walk back to the parking lot at PRBO.

AUDUBON CANYON GRIFFIN/BOURNE TRAIL LOOP

• Restrooms and water at Audubon Canyon Ranch only • Carry binoculars

DIRECTIONS: From the town of Point Reyes Station head south over the green bridge on Highway #1. About 12 miles down, the road splits: the right leg goes to Bolinas, the left goes to Stinson Beach. Bear left, around the lagoon, for a mile and a half. You will see the signs for Audubon Canyon Ranch on your left. Turn in at the first driveway and proceed SLOWLY to the parking area. About 13 miles from Point Reyes Station.

This trail is open to the public when the Audubon Canyon Ranch opens—mid-March to mid-July. Park in the parking area to the south of the ranch house. Follow the signs to the Griffin Trail and the rookery overlook. You will climb up the canyon through *oak* and *bay* forest. There's a lovely overlook just a short ways up the trail where you get a bird's-eye view of the Bolinas Lagoon and Bolinas mesa to the west. About an eighth of a mile further up, through the woods, you will pass the Henderson Overlook, where people gather to view the *heron* and *egret* rookery down below. The trail begins to climb steeply through old forest and then levels off about a mile past the overlook at the back of the canyon. A beautiful creek rushes steeply down through the canyon here where *ferns, yellow monkey flower, forget-me-nots* and other spring wildflowers abound.

The trail now traverses the north-facing side of the canyon where the moisture-loving *redwoods* stand. Leaving these woods, you climb through dense chaparral and arrive at another overlook for Bolinas Lagoon. The trail then merges with the Bourne trail, leading down from the top of the ridge, and heads through the grassland to the Audubon Canyon Ranch below. The open views are wonderful here, giving a real sense of the geography.

Once down into the clearing at the ranch you can rest on the grass or enjoy a picnic at one of the picnic tables on the grounds. You can leave a contribution at the desk in the bookstore for your use of the trail.

LAST NOTES: Because of the herds of dramatic tule elk, the Tomales Point Trail is a good one for older kids. Include the self-guided tour at Pierce Point Ranch. Bear Valley Trail offers varied sights and excellent prospects for seeing wildlife close up. Limantour Spit, out to the end and down to the edge of the estero, can be engrossing for older kids. *Harbor seals, white pelicans, egrets*, and *herons* are likely sights. Coast Trail to Bass Lake is challenging and varied for older children, with a lake or even a waterfall as rewards for making it to the end.

Read previous sections of this chapter for full descriptions of these trails— and happy hiking !

©1995 Ane Rovetta

A Shiny, Slimy Story

Story & Illustration by
Ane Rovetta

I n the old days the trees grew thicker and deeper than they do now. The ground was rich and wet and so steamy that the air was like a thick, clear syrup. Then the sun heaved itself above the mists. It tried to shine upon the thick green forest carpet, but the light could not reach through all that wetness. Instead, it just dazzled off the tops of the trees, then fell into thick golden drops. Some of those drops stretched their way down, down, down, becoming long and thin. They oozed through the air until they settled in long lines on the fertile soil.

For the longest time they lay still, until slowly, soft peaks pulled out of their heads and they began to quiver. Then, slowly, those slimy ones began to creep, belly first, crawling through the green. They had become the slow and splendid banana slugs, sliding from the beginning of time into our lives.

©1995 Ane Rovetta

FIELD NOTES

FIELD NOTES

Child Park Visitor with Ranger in Kule Loklo Village *Coast Live Oak Border*
· © 1995 Karen Gray

Chapter 5

Special Places in the Park for Children

DIRECTIONS: For directions refer to Chapter #2 - "Getting Your Bearings: Research and Education Centers - Bear Valley Visitor Center" on page 10.

KULE LOKLO INDIAN VILLAGE

As you walk the trail leading away from the parking lot at the Bear Valley Visitor Center to Kule Loklo you head up the hill through over-arching *coast live oak* and *bay* trees. At the top of the hill the trail cuts through a dense stand of *eucalyptus*. You emerge, magically, into a Coast Miwok village set in a clearing sheltered by hills and trees with magnificent views of the mountains to the east.

This is Kule Loklo, "Bear Valley," a recreated Coast Miwok village. A number of "kotchas," or houses, and other traditional structures have been painstakingly built over the years here by Coast Miwok and Pomo Native American people, park personnel and dedicated volunteers. There are tule kotchas, redwood bark kotchas, a shade structure of woven willow trees, granaries, and a traditional sweat lodge and ceremonial house. This last structure, built of barked saplings and covered over in earth, is kept locked unless park staff or volunteers are working in the area. It is occasionally used for Miwok ceremonies.

Children can enter the houses as they choose. It is a revealing experience to sit or lie inside these simply elegant structures and imagine the life of the people who lived in such places for thousands of years. The scale of the homes and familiarity of the building materials are in sharp contrast to the scale and exotic materials of our own homes. Our children can easily imagine a bustling village of elders, adults and youngsters going about their daily business of hunting, gathering, cooking, weaving, making clothes and, of course, playing.

On weekends in the spring and fall there are classes in traditional California Indian skills: making arrow points, bow making, arrow making, native plant uses, basketry and cordage. Story telling is also done in the village on some weekends. There is an annual Strawberry Festival the first Saturday in April that celebrates the Miwok people's culture and the coming of spring. The Big Time Festival is held the third weekend in July with dancing, crafts and traditional food. Call the Bear Valley Visitor Center for information (415) 663-1092.

The Miwok, who for about 8,000 years settled in villages like this one, lived their lives around the seasons using their fine skills in hunting, gathering and fishing. They hunted with bow and arrow as well as with intricately made traps for birds, rabbits and deer. Fish were caught with carefully fashioned dip nets, woven surf nets, and traps made of woven willow. They also fished as we do with pole and line. Coast Miwok people gathered the great bounty that Mother Nature served up year round: acorns, buckeye seeds, grass seed and plant bulbs, hazel nuts and bay nuts. At the ocean they gathered seaweeds and kelp, crab, mussels, abalone, limpets and oysters for eating fresh, or for smoking and drying for later. Ocean surf fish and rock fish were caught. Freshwater fish were abundant in the streams and lakes.

While the skins of animals were used for clothing and tools, the sinew was used for lacing and fastening arrowheads to shafts; bones were used for awls, hair pins and fish hooks. Shell was fashioned into ornaments and cut into pierced discs that were polished and strung for use in trading and money.

Both Bear Valley Visitor Center and the Ken Patrick Visitor Center at Drake's Beach have good exhibits explaining the life of the Coast Miwok in Point Reyes. Beautiful examples of basketry, clothing and tools are on display. For more extensive study, there are excellent books available in both bookstores that describe the Miwok's life and tell their stories. The Marin Museum of the American Indian located at 2200 Novato Boulevard in Novato is an excellent place to spend a rainy afternoon and learn more about these native

Californians. Call for more information: (415) 897-4064. The California wing of the Oakland Museum is another excellent place to study California Miwok.

MORGAN HORSE RANCH

You can see the Morgan Horse Ranch from the Bear Valley Visitor Center. Its open pasture is the hill directly behind the building. The ranch buildings are up the drive, hidden in the trees just west of the visitor center.

The little office building on your right as you enter the ranch complex is often staffed by a ranger. However, if there isn't anybody around, the stables, tack room, and historical display barn are well developed for self-guided tours. Antique farm machinery is displayed on the grass. In the little red barn on the left, there are historical photos and explanations of the development of the Morgan horse breed, as well as current snapshots of the Morgans at the park.

A large horse training ring is often in use by the volunteers and staff. The pasture just past the tack room and stables is equipped with all sorts of obstacles and training apparatus to familiarize the younger horses with their duties in the maintenance of the Seashore. Because the wilderness areas within the Seashore are closed to motorized vehicles, horses are used out on the trails for repair and maintenance work as well as trail patrols. There is often a young colt or two born here in the spring.

Barn swallows build their wonderful mud nests in the eaves of these buildings. In the spring there is a great commotion with parents swooping in and out to feed their young while the chicks huddle together with their faces peering out ready to be the first to get fed some delicious morsel. The nests are not very high up, so children can get a good view of these beautiful creatures.

A well-situated picnic table on the grass in front of the training ring is sheltered from wind. If you take the trail back around behind the training ring, you will skirt the fenced pasture, walking through dense *oak* and *bay*, and come out at Kule Loklo.

The park hosts the public on Morgan Horse Ranch Day in March of every year. Park interpreters explain the breed and give demonstrations of the Morgans at work clearing trails and working around obstacles. Children are introduced to particular horses that they can approach and pet.

Wheezy, Breezy Wings

Story & Illustration
by Ane Rovetta

I n the old days, flowers always had a cold. They would sniffle, and their centers would turn red. They would wheeze and cough, but somehow they didn't know how to sneeze! Caterpillar felt sorry for them. He would curl his fuzzy body around their stems like a warm, woolly scarf trying to help them, until finally he had an idea. He curled up and made himself into a cocoon, right on top of flower.

He stayed there all winter, but when spring came he began to wiggle and twitch and work his way out of his cocoon. All that itching and twitching made flower go ahhh, ahhh, ahhh.... CHOO! She blew that little insect high into the sky, and on each side of his body two flower petals were stuck there. They flapped and fluttered and hovered over him - he had become a butterfly !

So, now, every spring, caterpillars help the flowers to sneeze their winter colds out. And flowers reward them by blowing them high into the air with bright petals stuck to their sides. Breezy, wheezy butterflies appear all over the hillsides.

DOUGLAS FIR GROVE WITH
ACORN WOODPECKERS

Across the entry road from the Bear Valley Visitor Center is a grove of towering *Douglas fir* trees, home to a raucous colony of *acorn woodpeckers.* Their coarse yelling, "Jacob! Jacob! Jacob!" can be heard throughout the valley as they call to each other during a busy day's work. You will see them swoop from one tree trunk to another in a flash of black-and-white stripes, or spot them intently hopping up and around the tree trunks with their red-topped heads bobbing.

If you walk into the grove (which is also the picnic area, with humans happily pursuing their pleasures in the understory while the woodpeckers occupy the upper branches), you will have a chance to study the granaries of these industrious creatures. Thousands of holes have been drilled in the rough outer bark of the fir trees, each a perfect storage locker for an acorn from the *coast live oaks* nearby. The woodpeckers begin harvesting these in August, carefully bringing them up in their beaks to be hammered into place in just the right sized container for storage into the winter. If the squirrels and scrub jays haven't stolen them, many of these acorns will be retrieved by the woodpeckers in the lean cold months ahead for nourishment from the worms that live inside.

The woodpeckers carry on their business quite oblivious of the people far below them, which provides a great chance for children to observe the birds at length. Unlike many opportunities for studying wildlife involving lots of 'shushing' and admonitions for 'quiet!', these guys are just about as rambunctious as your children. If you bring a picnic or a snack and plan to sit a spell, the kids can find ample opportunity to satisfy their curiosity without feeling muzzled. Field glasses and a bird guide would be added bonuses.

NOTE: Wheelchair accessible

©1995 Ane Rovetta

PIERCE POINT RANCH SELF-GUIDED TOUR

DIRECTIONS: From the town of Point Reyes Station head south on Highway #1 for 2 miles. At the flashing stoplight in Olema take a left onto Sir Francis Drake Boulevard heading east. Go up and over Olema hill. In about 2 miles you will see the sign for the Cross Marin Trailhead. Turn left following the marker and park on the roadside. The trail begins here, leading underneath Sir Francis Drake Boulevard and into the redwood trees. Trailhead about 4 miles from Point Reyes Station.

Out at the end of Pierce Point Ranch Road on the northern tip of the Point Reyes Peninsula is the Pierce Point Ranch. Once a thriving dairy, it was also an independent and isolated community made up of the owner's family, dairy workers and their children. It even supported its own school for the children of the ranch and fishermen's kids who lived in the coves nearby on Tomales Bay. The park has restored many of the buildings and placed interpretive stations with illustrations and descriptions of the life on the ranch all around the site.

Like Kule Loklo, it doesn't take a big stretch of the imagination to picture life in this remote settlement. Pierce Point Ranch is a dramatic example of old rural California life and architecture for children to paint, draw and study. The barn is enormous and unlit so its cool, dank inside is a mysterious adventure. I am sure there are barn owls and bats back up in the rafters, but you can't see them in the dark.

There's a picnic table for visitors in the ranch yard. The nearest rest rooms are just down the road at the trailhead for McClure's Beach. The self-guided tour around the compound is on level hard ground good for wheelchairs and strollers. The interpretive plaques are well placed for chair-level reading.

The park hosts Dairy Day at the ranch in May. Call the Bear Valley Visitor Center for information at (415) 663-1092.

TULE ELK PRESERVE

DIRECTIONS: From the town of Point Reyes Station head south on Highway #1 for 2 miles. At the flashing stoplight in Olema take a left onto Sir Francis Drake Boulevard heading east. Go up and over Olema hill. In about 2 miles you will see the sign for the Cross Marin Trailhead. Turn left following the marker and park on the roadside. The trail begins here, leading underneath Sir Francis Drake Boulevard and into the redwood trees. Trailhead about 4 miles from Point Reyes Station.

The sight of these magnificent beasts at home in the Point Reyes landscape is an electrifying one. The racks of the males are very large and wide. You wonder how they manage to hold their heads up all day. Their muscular bodies with heart-shaped white rumps are impressive. I have never heard a male 'bugling' in the breeding season, but I've been told it's really something.

©1995 Ane Rovetta

For the best chance of seeing the *tule elk*, stop at the north side of Pierce Point Ranch Road and walk out to the marked viewpoint with interpretive map. From here you can often spot a group of elk. As the road dips down to the ranch, go slowly and keep an eye out in both directions. The elk herds are frequently lounging in the scrub, not far away. The best way to see elk is to hike out the Tomales Point Trail behind Pierce Point Ranch and get away from cars entirely. The elk range all over the point. Keep your eyes peeled - they are well camouflaged.

If your little ones are just learning to use binoculars or a spotting scope, tule elk are the perfect subject for location and observation. They are often just off in the landscape, close enough to spot with the naked eye. They stay pretty still, either grazing lazily or lounging in the grass. Recently, out on the point, my son (then just three-and-a-half) was thrilled to spot a herd of elk about two hundred feet away. He stayed in place on the trailside for some time getting them in focus and studying them in his field glasses. This was also the perfect chance to use our field guide to North American mammals. He was able to identify the elk himself by the color illustration and I could read the description of the animal and habitat to him. We've talked about tule elk with familiarity and awe ever since.

Once abundant in coastal Marin during the 1800s, the tule elk were hunted to near extinction for their tallow, meat and hides. Along with the European settlers came the foreign annual grasses that crowded out the native perennial bunchgrasses on which the elk were dependent. The California Gold Rush years, from 1849 on, saw a huge migration of people who poured into San Francisco and Sacramento looking for food and supplies before they headed out to the Mother Lode to find their fortunes in gold. Elk were hunted all over as an excellent meat for market, and the herds took to California's extensive marshes for cover, hiding amongst the tules - hence, their name.

The Park Service brought in two bull elk and eight cows as breeding stock to build a new population of the tule elk in the late 1970s. Since then, the elk have flourished with over one hundred animals now roaming the coastal scrub and grasslands of Tomales Point.

Only the males have those impressive antlers. They begin to grow in the spring and the velvet that covers the tender new growth is shed in the summer. By the time the velvet is rubbed off, the antlers are hard bone, ready for the competitive battle that will decide which male is dominant and wins the pleasure of the female's company. And, not just one female. One tule elk bull can shepherd as many as sixty cows in his harem. The calves are born in April and May and stay dependent on their mothers for four months. They are then weaned and begin to feed with the herd. These large animals graze on a varied diet of available herbs, grasses, acorns, tule, and reeds.

POINT REYES LIGHTHOUSE

DIRECTIONS: From Point Reyes Station, take Highway #1 south over the green bridge. Take an immediate right onto Sir Francis Drake Boulevard. Follow Sir Francis Drake through the town of Inverness and over the hill (at the "Y" in the road, stay left). Through the dairy ranches, past the turn-offs for Drake's Beach and Point Reyes beaches North and South you go past the turn-off for Chimney Rock, clear to the dead end of Sir Francis Drake Boulevard (about 45 minutes from town). Park in the lot for the lighthouse and walk 1/8 mile to the visitor center and top of the stairs for the lighthouse. About 20 miles from Point Reyes Station.

Perched at the western tip of the Point Reyes Peninsula (the western-most point on the continental United States), the Point Reyes Lighthouse was once vital to the safety of all sea craft that entered or left San Francisco Bay. Because it juts ten miles out into the Pacific Ocean, the point's rocky cliffs can be a treacherous obstacle to any boat navigating the fierce winds and blinding fogs of Point Reyes' waters. The lighthouse stood watch and gave

warning from the windiest point on the Pacific coast. The gate above
the 300 steps that lead down the cliffs to the lighthouse is often closed
to the public because of dangerous winds. (I have driven out to the point on days that
weren't so bad inland to find that I couldn't open my car door for the wind on the bluffs.)
For this reason, it is always wise to check conditions with the rangers at the Lighthouse
Visitor Center before driving the 45 minutes out to the point. (415) 669-1534. Closed
Tuesdays and Wednesdays.

      The lighthouse is a beautiful historical structure built in 1870. It did its job through
the dedication of a lone lighthouse keeper and three assistants who lit the oil lamps that
sent the lighthouse beam out one half-hour before sunset and extinguished it at sunrise.
In between, the assistants had to tend the wicks of the lamps, making sure that they didn't
burn out or give off soot that would dim the lenses. Sometimes the winds were so fierce on
the point that the keeper had to crawl back to his quarters so as not to be blown off the
steps that cascade down to the lighthouse from the bluff above.

      After 105 years of watchful guard, the lighthouse was retired when the Coast
Guard installed an automated light at Point Reyes. Then the lighthouse was turned over to
the National Park Service for
preservation as a valuable part of
our cultural heritage. The park
often sponsors events at the
lighthouse, with tours of the lantern
room and night lighting programs. Pick up the free
brochure "The Historic Point Reyes Lighthouse" from the
visitor center for details.

GRAY WHALE MIGRATION
POINT REYES, TOMALES POINT

      The migration of the *gray whale* is a magical seasonal event that draws people to
the Point Reyes Peninsula from all over the world. The unique location of the peninsula -
reaching so far out into the Pacific Ocean - makes it an extraordinary spot for viewing the
whales as they follow their annual route from the Arctic Sea to the waters off Baja, Mexico
and back again - a cycle of nearly 10,000 miles.

The southern migration begins to reach Point Reyes in late November. As the numbers of whales swell, sightings of these magnificent animals can reach a hundred a day; they peak around New Year's Day. Pregnant females traveling south will give birth to their calves in the warm, sheltered waters of the western lagoons and Sea of Cortez off Baja, California.

By February, the earliest whales travelling back north again will be spotted. Mothers will be travelling with their newborns somewhat later, around March and April. All these times vary somewhat, however, from year to year. More than ten thousand whales will migrate past Point Reyes in a season.

As the whales move along they come very near the point, often just a hundred feet away from the cliffs. The details of their flukes, barnacled backs and blow holes can be clearly visible. It's a thrilling sight. Sometimes, it's even a thrilling sound because the "whoosh!" of the whale's breathing can be clearly heard above on a still day.

The most popular spot for viewing the whales is the Point Reyes Lighthouse. This is where you can count on getting the closest look. The area is open from 10:00 a.m. to 4:30 p.m. and closes for windy weather. (The Lighthouse is closed on Tuesdays and Wednesdays.) During the peak season the park restricts car access out to this southern point, providing a shuttle bus for visitors that leaves frequently from North Beach.

Another great spot for whale watching is Tomales Point. Even if you just hike out a couple of miles you can get a fine view of the whales from the western bluffs adjacent to the Tomales Point Trail. The whales don't generally come in as close here but the quiet is wonderful and a pair of binoculars can give you a great view. The bluffs above Limantour Beach can be good for whale watching as well. Take the Limantour Road out and park in one of the pull-outs on the hills above the beach. Carry your binoculars.

Salmon Boy

Story by Jules Evens

Noah spots them first and points to some shoals at the end of a calm reach, just above the chattering riffles. Brawny backs — bronze and glistening — break the water's surface. We can see their flanks blushed red, their bodies nearly as long as the boys' outstretched arms. The salmon have returned. About ten of the old beasts face upstream, steadying themselves against the sway of the current with occasional tail-fanning and subtle body torques.

The creeks are running now, not bank full, but deep enough to flow smoothly across the reach, full enough to fold through the corrugated riffles. Later in the season the riffles will be drowned-out, but now, with the modest early season runoff, cobbles murmur and dimpled water winks silver motes of light through the forest. My nine-year-old son, Noah, his friend, Nick, and I walk down the footpath through the redwoods behind the ranger's kiosk. The shadows and the random flickering, the silence and the lapping gurgles, measure our pace. We follow the bank, deliberate as fly fishermen or foxes.

Salmon have been returning to this stretch of creek since before the first people built their first willow weirs, since before the first grizzly cub slapped the first gravid female onto the muddy shore, and maybe even before the first redwoods set their roots in these shadowy banks. The earliest Californians used to celebrate the return of the salmon with the Jump Dance, one of a cycle of rituals that made the world new each year.

Like grizzly cubs, Nick and Noah run straight into the water to catch the big red fish with their paws. I grab the boys by the scruffs of their necks and, appealing to their tender reason, try to convince them that this is not a good idea. I explain that this is the most important phase of the salmon's life cycle. If we disturb them now they might not be able to complete their ancestral rites and in a few years there might not be any fish left in the creek. More than a century of overfishing, logging, damming, water diversion, and siltation, coupled with the sparsity of rain these past six years, has made the salmon spawn a rare event. We are no longer free to act like grizzlies.

These fish are cold water, rain running, hooked-nosed, speckle backed, battle scarred, "silver salmon" - the embodiment of the North Pacific coast, the nerves of its streams. We call them "Coho" - Coho - an old sound that comes from deep in the chest, from somewhere near the center of our being. After spending two years in the Pacific, Coho return to their place of birth, fighting currents and curses no organism should have to endure. If they survive sharks, seals, and seines, baited hook lines, hungry bears and people, droughts, dammed rivers, and denuded watersheds, the struggle over sharp rocks and surging rapids, they find the same riffle or back eddy where they hatched a few years before.

The salmon spawn has spawned its own language, suiting its novelty. The nest is a "redd"; the physiological changes each fish undergoes from fresh water to salt water is "smolting"; the sperm of the male is "milt." The female makes her redd by lying on her side in the riffles and fanning her tail forcefully, "winnowing" a shallow depression in the gravel in which she lays a few hundred eggs. There, at the foot of the deep reach and just above the head of the riffles the water turbulence is ideal for aeration of the eggs. A male waits patiently nearby, then follows his mate and spreads his milt over the nest as the female moves slightly upstream to repeat the process. As she winnows the next redd, the sand and gravel drift down to bury the eggs in the previous nest, and so, upstream, they continue until they have laid, fertilized, and buried a few thousand roe. This will be the last effort of their lives. Spent, they then drift into a still shoal and die in a bed of willow and alder leaves, the calcium and cartilage of their bodies nourishing the next generation.

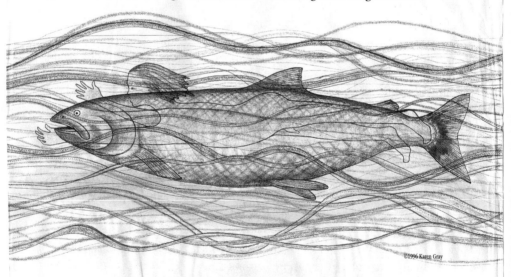

©1996 Karen Gray

Bear once waited here on this bank where we sit watching the winter salmon spawn. Now, we are quiet, empty of thoughts or feelings, unaware that we are fathers or sons, hunters or humans. A sliver of sun slices through the conifer canopy and shards of light shiver on the foliage. There is a soft sloshing in the still water and the clean smell of greenery. I tell the boys a story I heard on a recent trip up the Northwest Coast.

There was once a boy who caught more salmon than he or his family could eat. This habit caused him to be named "Too Many Fish." One day the salmon people snuck into the village, kidnapped Too Many Fish from his parents and took him to their village to raise him as their own. While living with the salmon, the boy learned their ways. Eventually, he turned into a salmon. After living with the salmon people for a few years, he swam back upriver to his old village. A woman was fishing on the bank and caught the boy-fish, whom she recognized as her long lost son. When she pulled him out of the water, he shed his salmon skin and emerged in human form. From then on he was known as Salmon Boy. Reunited with his family and his village, the boy taught his people the ways of the salmon. Through his teaching, they understood that one should only catch as many salmon as one's family needs and all the parts of the salmon that are not eaten - the bones, the fins, the eyes - should be returned to the river. When the boy grew to manhood, he became a village elder, a shaman. One day he was fishing in the creek and caught a beautiful salmon with translucent skin. Looking at the fish he realized that the salmon was actually his own soul. He then threw the fish back in the stream. The salmon spun around four times then disappeared under the water. As it swam away, the thrust of his tail left only a slight ripple on the surface.

Noah, Nick and I leave the spawning riffles and start our own Jump Dance downstream, skipping along slippery rocks. We expect to find the water swollen with more gravid salmon just around each next bend, but all we see are empty pools. "Too deep" or "too shallow," "not enough rapids!" my companions say with the unimpeachable conviction of instant experts.

I stop to catch my breath and I watch the salmon boys skip and balance downstream, rock to rock. In their exuberance they crowd one another off a too small rock and push one another into the shallow water, laughing and splashing. In the flickering forest light of this new world, I can almost see their souls bursting through their skins.

©1996 Jules Evens

SAMUEL P. TAYLOR STATE PARK
LAGUNITAS CREEK SALMON RUN

DIRECTIONS: Take Highway #1 south from Point Reyes Station. Go left at the flashing red light in the hamlet of Olema. Go about 4 miles east to the main entrance for Samuel P. Taylor State Park.

Every fall the King and Coho salmon native to this area swim back to their birth places from the open sea. They find their place of origin by smell, returning to just the place in the creek where they were hatched to lay and fertilize their eggs in the shallows before they die. There is a park service display near the little bridge that crosses the creek explaining their remarkable journey.

Call the ranger station at Samuel P. Taylor State Park for more information: (415) 488-9897.

LAGUNITAS CREEK WORK PARTY

Every year before the rains begin Trout Unlimited throws a wonderful work party on the banks of Lagunitas Creek in Samuel P. Taylor State Park. An organization of dedicated volunteers, Trout Unlimited has chapters across the country with members who make it their business to protect and restore fish habitat.

At Samuel P. Taylor, families come from all over the Bay Area to work together building fish ladders, planting riparian cover, cleaning debris out of the creek and doing whatever needs to be done to make the creek hospitable to spawning salmon. In true Marin County fashion, the event is catered by wonderful restaurants and bakeries who donate their efforts on behalf of the fishery.

If your family would like to help, you can call the ranger station at Samuel P. Taylor State Park: (415) 488-9897.

FIELD NOTES

Child & Goat Kid at Point Reyes Annual Livestock Show
©1995 Karen Gray

Chapter 6

Town Joys for Kids

THE DANCE PALACE COMMUNITY CENTER

The Dance Palace has been Point Reyes' center for culture and community life for more than twenty years. Originally housed in an old store front (previously called the "Dance Palace") on Main Street, where the Cabaline Saddle Shop and Bovine Bakery are now, the new community center is on B Street between 5th and 6th. The little white clapboard building was once the Catholic church for Point Reyes. The large central building was completed just a few years ago along with the Papermill Creek Children's Corner preschool next door.

If you just cruise by, you can check out the current offerings listed on the billboard at streetside. Through the main doors under the yellow archway you will find the monthly "Dance Palace Calendar of Events" on the table underneath the bulletin board. ("The Calendar of Events" is carefully coded to give you the information you need should you want to bring children to a particular event.) If the building is locked, you may call the Dance Palace information line and office at (415) 663-1075.

The community supports a summer stock players troupe of local children who do plays and musicals that are first rate, a children's chorus that is part of the West Marin Music Festival, and special events around the holidays for children. Concerts, story telling, plays, lectures and special events are constantly produced here. Many of these are especially geared to families and children. The Dance Palace hosts dramatic and musical groups from all over the world: puppeteers, choruses, dance troupes, trapeze performers - all kinds of entertainment.

The Dance Palace operates all year round and admission to events is nominal. There is wheelchair access throughout.

POINT REYES STATION FIRE HOUSE
FIRE TRUCKS

At the corner of 4th and B Streets is the West Marin Emergency Services building, which houses the local Sheriff's sub-station as well as the Point Reyes Fire House and Paramedics. The brown-shingle building has glass doors on the garage so the fire trucks can be viewed by little people at any time - unless, of course, a call comes in and then you'd better get out of the way, fast.

All our fire trucks are the old-fashioned bright red. Often the firemen have them out in the driveway for washing and polishing so you can get a close-up view.

Once a year in June the firemen host a benefit pancake breakfast. A banner goes up over the highway a few weeks in advance with the date. They pull out the trucks and fill the sunny garage with tables. Locals go and socialize and visitors are welcome. The firemen are excellent short-order cooks, too.

GIACOMINI DAIRY CALF CORRALS

At the corner of 6th and B Streets in Point Reyes Station is the calf corral for the Giacomini Dairy. The youngin's are kept here when they are weaned and separated from their mothers. Yellow tags in their ears identify them by number. They are fed in bins at the back of the corral every day.

If you walk up to the fence quietly they will come running like little puppies. They are very curious and playful. They will smell your hands and try to suck your fingers. Their large, intense faces with 'whooshing' breath may scare some little kids, but not mine. From the time he was just a few months old nothing could calm my son like a stroll down to the calves for a shared study session: they watched him intently and he watched them back.

NOTE: Do not tease these animals. Loud noises or throwing things is forbidden and poor behavior. Cows have feelings, too, you know.

TOMALES BAY COMMUNITY PLAYGROUND

Jane Senter, a local resident, had two small kids and no place for them to play with other kids near town. She organized her fellow parents and built the Tomales Bay Community Playground at the southern corner of the West Marin School grounds.

Just up Highway One about two blocks north of town on the right, the playground is sunny and sheltered. It has a picnic table and benches, a park bench, merry-go-round, baby swings, big kid swings and a big wooden play structure with two slides - one for little guys and a spiral one for bigger kids. The playground is there for all to enjoy. Keep the gate closed since it is right off the highway.

MOO COW CLOCK

If you are in downtown Point Reyes Station at noon time or six p.m. with a preschooler, the town 'cow clock' is good for a laugh. It's a loud recording of a mooing cow. For some reason, Judy Borello, owner of the Old Western Saloon, decided to install it on the top of her building. Twice a day at noon and six.

©1995 Ane Rovetta

AND FURTHER AFIELD...

THE ROUGE ET NOIR CHEESE FACTORY

If you take a right off of Highway #1 onto the Point Reyes-Petaluma Road just north of Point Reyes Station, you're on your way to the Cheese Factory. The road winds around Nicasio Reservoir and through a landscape of dairy and beef cattle before coming down into Hick's Valley, about nine miles from town. You will see the red-and-black sign for "Rouge et Noire" on your left. Pull in and park.

As long as you buy some cheese or other picnic supplies, you are welcome to use the beautiful picnic grounds around the pond. The factory gives tours throughout the day that can be fascinating for older children. The guides take you right inside the factory and explain the age-old method of making cheese as well as the history of the family that founded the place. The people are especially hospitable and welcoming to families.

The store in front of the cheese-making building sells picnic supplies, all their cheese plus fresh coffee and bread. You can buy food there or bring your own picnic. They will even give you stale bread to feed the ducks and geese on the pond if you forgot yours.

On a clear day this open valley is a thing of beauty. Surrounded by rolling pasture lands and cultivated fields, the picnic grounds around the pond have a clear view in all directions to the surrounding hillsides studded with *coast live oak.*

The rest rooms, store and picnic tables are wheelchair accessible.

©1995 Ane Rovetta

TOMALES BAY OYSTERS

Just up Highway #1 about 12 miles from Point Reyes Station is the little hamlet of Marshall. Historically a fisherman's village amid the surrounding dairy ranches, Marshall is home to a number of oyster farmers who lease portions of Tomales Bay in which to grow different varieties of shellfish. Tomales Bay Oyster Company is the one you will come to first. Perched on the side of the bay are just a few bright, white-washed buildings that house the workmen and the harvesting operation. You can walk right up to the holding tanks where they keep the recently harvested oysters and mussels alive in fresh water to sell. They are available by size and number, and are delicious.

We eat the oysters fresh with tabasco and lemon juice right there at the picnic table. Many people take them home to steam, fry or barbecue. My son loves them any way. Children can stand right out on the shell-strewn beach and feel the teaming life in the bay at their feet. On a sunny day, this spot is like a dream: sparkling azure water, bright blue sky, the lush Inverness Ridge right across the way, and the sound of water gently lapping on the shore. If they are not too busy, the harvesters (usually in their waist-high waders) will answer your questions about oyster farming.

The Hog Island Oyster Company is the next stop up the road, right in the hamlet of Marshall. Their holding tanks are also at bayside, around back of the old general store, now used as the Marshall Art Center. Locals often mount art shows, theater pieces, and musical events here. The holding tanks for shell fish are right above the shell-strewn beach.

Hog Island is especially proud of its "sweetwater" oysters that have a delicious flavor because of their growth at the mouth of Walker Creek, in a perpetual mix of salt and fresh water. They also grow and sell steamer clams (cockles) and abalone.

Hog Island provides a few picnic tables and barbecues for guests to use on pleasant days.

Children Fishing with Leopard Shark Catch   *Squid Border*
©1995 Karen Gray

Chapter 7

Gone Fishin':
What's Biting & Where

     Well, first let's talk about regulations and the law. Anybody under 16 can fish without a license so long as they obey all the rules and regulations about what you take where and how many and what size and so on. People sixteen years or older must have a valid California fishing license displayed on their person for the taking of any kind of fish, mollusk, invertebrate, amphibian, crustacean or reptile (except rattlesnakes). No amphibians or reptiles may be taken in the Point Reyes National Seashore. If you're even thinking about fishing, pick up a copy of the California Department of Fish and Game's "California Sport Fishing Regulations" along with your fishing license at the Building Supply Center in Point Reyes Station. Remember that the fees you pay for your license support wildlife protection and management throughout California. It's a good idea to carry the regulations with you since restrictions on sizes and numbers are very specific. (Carry a small measuring tape, too. What you think looks like 8" may not be.) Since you must now wear your license in plain view while fishing, you should ask for a clear plastic

©1995 Ane Rovetta

tube holder or zip-lock plastic bag with attaching pin to keep your license dry and displayed. (The paper that licenses are printed on these days is really tacky and doesn't hold up to moisture at all.) Needless to say, fishing regulations are very strictly enforced in the Point Reyes area since so much of it is National Seashore, National Marine Sanctuary, and State Park.

NOTE: POINT REYES HEADLANDS RESERVE and ESTERO DE LIMANTOUR RESERVE are wildlife reserves and all marine life is protected within their boundaries. In the DUXBURY REEF RESERVE only some invertebrates and fish can be taken.

Fishing in many of the creeks and streams within the national Seashore is prohibited. Refer to the color brochure on Point Reyes available for free from the visitor center for the boundaries of reserves. There are no public fishing piers within the National Seashore.

Frozen squid, frozen sardines and other small fish can be bought at Palace Market in Point Reyes Station and at the Inverness Store. Point Reyes Building Supply carries frozen bait, night crawlers and red worms. Mussels off the rocks make good bait for rock fish and eels. Carry a sharp knife for cutting the strong 'hairs' that hold the mussel in its colony. (Never pull a clump of mussels off the rock. This creates a hole in the colony that weakens its resistance to the powerful surf and endangers the others.)

Tackle and other gear can be bought at the Building Supply. They also carry life jackets, boots, rain hats, warm socks, bandannas, knives, poles and nets. Becker's Deli and the Inverness Store carry some tackle and bait.

It's virtually impossible to go fishing and keep your feet dry. Carry day packs so each of you can bring along your light weight sneakers and socks, maybe even a dry pair of pants, in a plastic bag. Fish in these, then change back into your warm dry clothes for the hike back to the car. An old five-gallon bucket to hold your bait and waterproof sunscreen are essential.

WARNING: If fishing on the Pacific Coast side, beware of incoming tides and sneaker waves. We put our son in a life jacket for safety when he's near the surf. Deep fishing boots are sensible for surf fishing on the beaches. They are not smart for fishing off the rocks - in case you should slip in, they simply fill with water and weight you

*down. An old pair of sneakers or, better yet, water booties, are ideal.
Teach your kids never to turn their backs on the ocean and always
keep a wary eye out for sneaker waves. Check the weather reports for storms at
sea and the tides before heading out on a fishing trip. Fish at your own risk.*

I have found that *A Field Guide to Pacific Coast Fishes* in the "Peterson Field Guide Series" is a valuable resource to take along. Pocket-guide size with excellent, detailed illustrations, the guide has extensive notes on particular fishes, often including information on how they are fished and whether they are good eating.

TOMALES BAY

TOMALES BAY has many beaches on both the east and west sides where you can fish for *redtail perch, leopard shark, striped bass, jack smelt* and *skate.* Leopard Shark is a delicious fish if skinned right away and grilled or fried fresh. The skate 'wings' must be cut from the body and skinned promptly. They are very good eating—so good that, years ago, we had a sly butcher in town who used a biscuit cutter on the wings and sold the round pieces as 'Pacific scallops.' He did real well with it.

MILLER PUBLIC PARK

DIRECTIONS: Take Highway #1 north out of Point Reyes Station. Go past the town of Marshall four miles and you will see the park on your left at bayside.

MILLER PARK PUBLIC FISHING ACCESS at Nick's Cove on Tomales Bay is a good spot for *perch, halibut* and *striped bass* fishing. The park has picnic tables, restrooms, a small jetty and a public fishing pier. (No fishing license is required on the pier. Licenses are required when fishing from the shore.) The park is open from 5 a.m. to 10 p.m. seven days a week. No fires allowed and pets must be leashed.

NOTE: Since most of the sandy coves along Tomales Bay are also used by swimmers, be especially careful to fish away from the swimming areas. Retrieve your snagged gear and hooks so as not to injure anyone who comes after you.

DRAKE'S BAY

DIRECTIONS: See Chapter #3 - "Where the Land Meets the Sea: The Beautiful Beaches, Drakes's Beach" - page 35.

DRAKE'S BAY is a favored spot for surf fishing. *Perch, flounder, sea trout, leopard shark* and *rockfish* are all caught here. A pole-holder that you can stick in the sand when your line is out is a real convenience for smaller kids who may tire of standing for long periods waiting for a bite. (A section of 4" PVC plumbing pipe about 30" long will work just fine.)

FRESH WATER FISHING

STAFFORD LAKE

Directions: Drive just north of Point Reyes Station on Highway #1. Take a right onto the Point Reyes-Petaluma Road. Follow it out 9 miles (past the Rouge et Noire Cheese Factory) to Novato Boulevard. Take that right to Novato for about five miles. You will see the entrance for Stafford Lake County Park on your right.

STAFFORD LAKE, just west of Novato, is stocked with *largemouth black bass* and *red-eared sunfish*. The limit is five bass per day. They must be 12" or more. Live bait is not allowed. The lake is surrounded by a beautiful park with large shade trees, picnic tables, barbecues, rest rooms, a children's playground and green grass. The lake is drinking water so no boating or bathing is allowed.

Park hours are 8 a.m. to sunset. There is a $1 per car day-use fee. No dogs are allowed in the park. for more information call: (415) 897-0618.

NICASIO RESERVOIR

DIRECTIONS: Drive just north of Point Reyes Station on Highway #1. Take a right onto the Point Reyes-Petaluma Road. At the intersection and stop sign take a left, keeping to the Point Reyes-Petaluma Road. In a few miles you will pass the spillway for the Nicasio Reservoir on your right. Half-a-mile further on you will see the sign for the Nicasio Reservoir and a blue porta-potty. The fishing coves begin along the shoreline here and continue around to the eastern side of the lake, off Nicasio Valley Road. (Take hats and warm jackets - the wind can be fierce here.)

     NICASIO RESERVOIR is just east of Point Reyes Station about six miles. There are *catfish, largemouth black bass, crappie, bluegill* and *carp* in the lake. Fishing is best in the small coves off the road using worms or crappie jigs. There are porta-potties and roadside pull-outs for parking. No dogs allowed. This lake is drinking water so no boating or bathing is allowed.

FIELD NOTES

FIELD NOTES

Avocet on Beach *Kelp Border*
©1995 Karen Gray

Chapter 8

Messing About in Boats:
Kayaks, Canoes & Inflatables

"This has been a wonderful day!" said he, as the Rat shoved off and took to the sculls again. "Do you know, I've never been in a boat before in all my life."

"What?" cried the Rat, open-mouthed: "Never been in a — you never — well, I — what have you been doing, then?"

"Is it so nice as all that?" asked the Mole shyly, though he was quite prepared to believe it as he leant back in his seat and surveyed the cushions, the oars, the rowlocks, and all the fascinating fittings, and felt the boat sway lightly under him.

"Nice? It's the only thing," said the Water Rat solemnly, as he leaned forward for his stroke. "Believe me, my young friend, there is nothing — absolutely nothing — half so much worth doing as simply messing about in boats. Simply messing......."

-from The Wind in the Willows
by Kenneth Grahame

The world of Point Reyes opens up in an entirely new way when you go exploring in a boat. Many rocky coves and beaches can only be reached by water. The creeks and estuaries allow you to travel the trail systems used by the wildlife down at their level: water level. Gliding silently in a canoe amongst the tules and grasses may bring to mind Longfellow's Hiawatha and Minihaha on the banks of the Gitchigumi. On the water, isolated from the sights and sounds of cars, today's children can feel themselves a part of Mother Nature in a unique way. The profound quiet of the water is mysterious. Surprises await you behind every log and blind curve.

Bobbing around in the shallows of a cove on Tomales Bay in a rubber inflatable, you get a view back at the landscape and the people on the beach that you can't get any other way. If you look overboard you might see scores of jellyfish propelling gracefully through the waters of the bay or a harbor seal pop its head up nearby, glassy eyes watching you as a whiskered snout struggles to pick up your scent - then it vanishes under water.

HEART'S DESIRE BEACH

DIRECTIONS: See Chapter #3 "Where the Land Meets the Sea: The Beautiful Beaches, Perfect for Toddlers -- Heart's Desire Beach," page 28.

HEART'S DESIRE BEACH is an ideal place to put in with any craft *(no motors!)*. You can drive right up to beachside, so you never have to haul your gear very far. The beach is pretty shallow with few sharp rocks. The cove itself is quite protected from the prevailing winds that howl down the bay some days.

From here you can skirt the shoreline in either direction - north or south - stopping in coves to explore and watching the land for wildlife.

LIMANTOUR ESTERO

DIRECTIONS: See Chapter #3 - "Where the Land Meets the Sea: The Beautiful Beaches - Limantour Beach" page 36.

LIMANTOUR ESTERO is a wonderful spot for kayaks and canoes. Park in the main Limantour Beach parking lot on the right at the end of the road. Portage your boat down the trail to the west and right of the paved trail that crosses the marsh. Here is a path through the *pickleweed* that will take you down to the water's edge at high tide. The estero waters are shallow, so you may spot all kinds of vegetation and wildlife over the side. Depending on the time of year, numerous waterfowl are here including the striking *white pelicans* that congregate on the eastern shore of the estero in the winter. Over on this side as well, you may notice the beach strewn with silver-gray "logs" that move: these are the *harbor seals* that haul out in the shelter of the estero for rest and sunshine.

WARNING: Limantour Estero is closed to boating each year from March 15th through June 30th to protect the harbor seal pupping areas. No boats or kayaks are allowed. At other times: please be respectful of all these creatures. Don't approach near enough to cause them to fuss and move about, and never make loud noises that will disturb them.

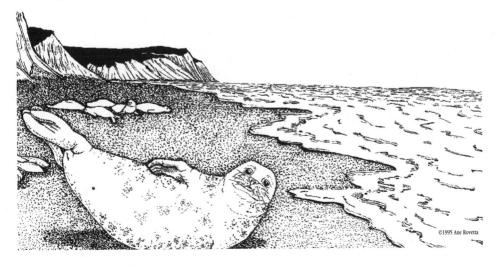

©1995 Ane Rovetta

PAPERMILL CREEK

DIRECTIONS: From Point Reyes Station head south on Highway #1. Just over the green bridge take an immediate right onto Sir Francis Drake Boulevard. Follow this about one mile. As the road turns broadly right you will see a large pull-out and bus stop sign on the right. Park here, past the bus stop, and look for the short trail down to the water's edge.

PAPERMILL CREEK at White House Pool is a terrific spot - the reeds are tall, the road is hidden high above you, the channels are narrow and mysterious. From here you can go upstream, under the green bridge and quite a ways further, depending on time of year and the tide. A seasonal gravel dam sometimes blocks access up to the bridge. It is a ponding device for the Giacomini Dairy Ranch that borders the creek for miles. You can also go downstream towards Tomales Bay and through the many channels that course through the reeds. This is the place where fresh water meets salt, so a great variety of wild animals can be observed here.

 WARNING: Depending on the season, the tides in the bay can be very swift and powerful. Always carry your tide book and wristwatch. Pay attention to days with very high and low tides when the waters will be moving with greatest force. Time your outings so that you avoid having to paddle in against the tide — you will be tired and you will want to have the water as a help rather than a hindrance. Be aware also that the southern end of Tomales Bay can turn to mud flats at low tide. This is not a funny circumstance — getting stranded in the goo that will hold your craft in place but refuse to support your body ashore can be very unpleasant. It's a long, cold wait for the tide to come in again.

LAST REMINDER: The people and wildlife of Point Reyes need quiet for their survival. NO motorized craft in these areas allowed.

The afternoon sun was getting low as the rat sculled gently homewards in a dreamy mood, murmuring poetry-things over to himself, and not paying much attention to Mole. But the Mole was very full of lunch, and self-satisfaction and pride, and already quite at home in a boat (so he thought) and was getting a bit restless besides: and presently he said, "Ratty! Please, I want to row, now!"

The Rat shook his head with a smile. "Not yet, my young friend," he said, "wait till you've had a few lessons. It's not so easy as it looks."

The Mole was quiet for a minute or two. But he began to feel more and more jealous of Rat, sculling so strongly and so easily along, and his pride began to whisper that he could do it every bit as well. He jumped up and seized the sculls, so suddenly, that the Rat, who was gazing out over the water and saying more poetry-things to himself, was taken by surprise and fell backwards off his seat with his legs in the air for the second time, while the triumphant Mole took his place and grabbed the sculls with entire confidence.

"Stop it, you silly ass!" cried the Rat, from the bottom of the boat. "You can't do it! You'll have us over!"

The Mole flung his sculls back with a flourish, and made a great dig at the water. He missed the surface altogether, his legs flew up above his head, and he found himself lying on the top of the prostrate Rat. Greatly alarmed, he made a grab at the side of the boat, and the next moment - Sploosh!

Over went the boat, and he found himself struggling in the river.

O my, how cold the water was, and O, how very wet it felt. How it sang in his ears as he went down, down, down! How bright and welcome the sun looked as he rose to the surface coughing and spluttering! How black was his despair when he felt himself sinking again! Then a firm paw gripped him by the back of his neck. It was the Rat, and he was evidently laughing - the Mole could feel him laughing, right down his arm and through his paw, and so into his - the Mole's - neck.

-from Wind in the Willows
by Kenneth Grahame

SAFETY FIRST!
WEAR YOUR LIFE JACKETS! and HAPPY BOATING!

Osprey's Boldness

Story & Illustration
by Ane Rovetta

O sprey loved to fly up high in the sky. His friends often warned him that flying too high is dangerous, that he might forget something. He might forget that he belongs to the earth! Because flying is a gift. It is a gift that bird people have only as long as they remember the Earth.

But Osprey, he kept his head in the clouds, he couldn't hear his friends, way down below him.

Osprey just circled, higher and higher until he scraped against something. It was the top of the sky! His head hit it so hard, it flattened a little bit, and it knocked him back... It bumped him so hard he started falling, right towards the sun! In that bright light he could hardly see, but he was able to swerve just in time... He swooped away. Only the sides of his face and the backs of his wings were scorched black.

But his adventure changed him. To this day that beautiful white Osprey shines as bright as the sun as he circles in the sky. But as soon as he is high enough he dives straight down into the water. He wants to make sure that the fire is put out.

FIELD NOTES

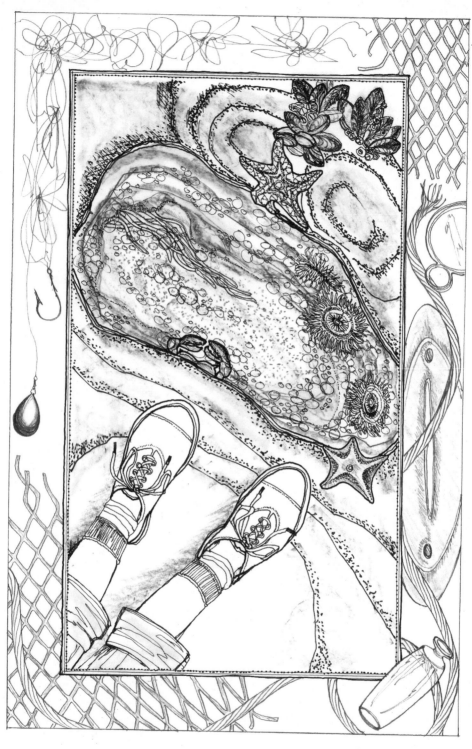

Child in Sneakers at Tide Pool *Flotsam and Jetsam Border*
©1995 Karen Gray

Chapter 9

Just Looking:
The Amazing World of Tide Pools

The scale of tide pools with their variety of colorful creatures is custom-tailored for children. A whole world of water animals is contained in a single pool shimmering at their feet. The longer they look, the more they will see. Ever-changing with the rushing waves, these perfect communities are a fascinating web of prey and predator, solitary animals and tight colonies, varied sea weeds and the creatures that hide in them, all beautifully camouflaged.

In your backpack, carry a pair of old sneakers and socks (or better yet, a pair of water booties) that you can change into when you reach the tide pools. Tidepooling is best done at minus tides. Check your tide book (or daily paper) and arrive and hour or so early in order to have plenty of time to explore and study before the sea comes in again. (Don't forget to make the time adjustment from the Golden Gate Bridge to Point Reyes - the tide book tells you how.)

A hand lens for observing detail, watercolors, colored pencils, and drawing paper are

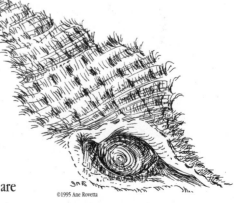

©1995 Ane Rovetta

wonderful tools for observation at tide pools. Cameras and field guides add more depth to your family's understanding of who these creatures are and how they live: why is that little crab inside a snail's shell? Why is that orange sea star wrapped around those mussels on the rock? What does that turquoise sea anemone, waving in the flowing water like a delicate flower, eat, anyway, and how?

    Seashore Life on Rocky Coasts published by the Monterey Bay Aquarium is an excellent guide to throw in your pack. Illustrated in rich color photographs, the text covers our most common tide pool creatures as well as an overview of the intertidal zone and how this community survives.

MᶜCLURE'S BEACH

    McCLURE'S BEACH offers wonderful tide pooling. After hiking down the trail to the beach, turn left heading south. You will see the rock outcroppings down the beach waiting for you. Numerous walls of inhabited rock as well as tide pools are easily observed here. If the tide is especially low and you are early (providing you allow enough time to get back before the tide comes in and closes off the access), clamber over the polished granite boulders in the opening to the south. You will come out onto a secluded little cove that faces due south. There are large rocks set in the sandy bottom whose walls host a colorful variety of *mussels, barnacles, orange* and *purple sea stars, crabs, periwinkles, limpets* and *seaweeds.*

CHIMNEY ROCK

    CHIMNEY ROCK also has great tide pools. After parking in the main parking lot at the road's end, walk down the hill to the little paved road on the Drake's Bay side of the promontory. This road leads along the shore to the old Life Boat Station, recently restored. You can peek in the windows and see the life boat inside on its sled, ready to slip down the tracks into the bay. Walk past the station down to the beach and rocks beyond. Here you will be fairly sheltered from prevailing winds and can explore the beautiful coves and pools that edge the bay.

NOTE: Bring study gear with you - such as a hand lens, camera, and drawing supplies - that will allow your kids to explore the tide pool community without unnecessarily touching or moving creatures. Tide pool animals are intricately woven into their niche by Mother Nature and are easily stressed by handling and displacement. If you do pick a creature up, put it back in the same spot.

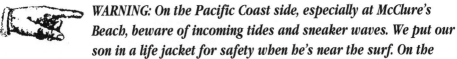

WARNING: On the Pacific Coast side, especially at McClure's Beach, beware of incoming tides and sneaker waves. We put our son in a life jacket for safety when he's near the surf. On the beach an old pair of sneakers or, better yet, water booties, are ideal. Teach your kids never to turn their backs on the ocean and always keep a wary eye out for sneaker waves. Check the weather reports for storms at sea and the tides.

Mother & Child Watching Moonrise over Tomales Bay *Flying Bats Border*
©1995 Karen Gray

Chapter 10

Beautiful Sunsets, Moonrises & Where to See the Stars

LOOKING WESTWARD

Sunsets in Point Reyes can be spectacular. They can also be invisible, since the fog may roll in and obscure the sun entirely before it completes its daily rounds. Just remember to stay loose and ready for what Mother Nature gives you, even if it isn't what you'd planned.

MOUNT VISION

DIRECTIONS: See "Chapter #4 - Hit the Trail!" page 53 for directions. Mt. Vision is the turn-off just before the Estero Trail turn-off.

Halfway up the mountain is a large pull-out with a viewpoint that looks out over the pasturelands and the western beaches below. This can be a lovely place to view the sunset over the Pacific. There is a hard shoulder and wheelchair access.

UPDATE: The Mt. Vision area burned in the Mt. Vision fire of October 1995. Watch for spectacular spring wildflower displays and dramatic changes in vegetation.

KEHOE BEACH

DIRECTIONS: See Chapter #3 - "Where the Land Meets the Sea: The Beautiful Beaches" page 32 for directions.

If you can hike a ways, walk out the trail to Kehoe Beach, and take the spur up to the right that leads over the bluffs. You will come out on rolling hills that make you feel as though you're floating out over the Pacific, with the gulls and turkey vultures at eye level. From here you can look down on the beaches and out to the sunset on the horizon. You can see south to the lighthouse on the point and north quite a ways to Elephant Rock, just beyond McClure's Beach.

ESTERO TRAIL

DIRECTIONS: See Chapter #4 - "Hit the Trail!" page 53 for directions.

If you are prepared for a longer hike, walk out the Estero Trail past the footbridge. Follow the trail up the steep grade and around the hill about two and a half miles until you come out on the bluff with the old *eucalyptus* tree that overlooks Drake's Estero. You'll be rewarded with a beautiful play of light on the rolling landscape and the waters of the Estero as the sun goes down. Carry your flashlights for the walk back in the dark. Keep a careful ear open for the calls of *owls* as you pass through the *pine* woods. Especially with a full moon, when you can see better, you may spot the owls gliding over the water between the two *pine* woods. If you're lucky you may see one heading out on its nocturnal foray over the hillsides in search of prey.

ALL PACIFIC BEACHES

If you prefer your sunsets at the beach, of course, all of the west-facing beaches are ideal to view the sun slipping into the water with the sound of the surf at your feet.

LOOKING EASTWARD TO THE MOONRISE

BOLINAS RIDGE TRAIL

DIRECTIONS: Head south out of Point Reyes Station on Highway #1. At the intersection of Highway #1 and Sir Francis Drake Boulevard in Olema turn left heading east on Sir Francis Drake. Go up the hill about a mile and when the road begins to drop down watch for the pull-out on the right with a trail marker at the wooden stile. Park here and head up the old ranch road about half a mile.

Moonrises in Point Reyes can be exquisite. One of our family's favorite spots is up the Bolinas Ridge Trail out of Olema. You will be gaining altitude pretty fast along this steep stretch. When you get to the intersection with the Jewell Trail, there is a large granite outcropping down the slope on your left. (Beware of *poison oak* on the granite outcroppings.) As you climb out onto it you'll find a level spot that feels like a fairy ring in the moonlight. This is large enough for an evening picnic while you wait for Luna's first golden light to appear over the hilltops. If you're not up to hiking quite this far there are a few hillsides only a quarter-mile out on the trail that are lovely for viewing as well. Carry your flashlights for the walk back. Do not disturb the cattle.

Bat Shapes the World

Story & Illustratrion
by Ane Rovetta

I n the old days, the world was just mud. It was soggy and flat. Darkness covered everything and it was so heavy it pushed everything down. Nothing could live. The plants tried to grow but darkness pushed them down. It made their leaves flat.

Bat was there. He was wiggling in the mud. He couldn't get up, that darkness was pushing him down. He tried to lift his head to the sky, but the darkness pushed his nose in and made his face all wrinkled. Bat felt afraid because he was all alone, but he had great heart inside of him. So he spread his fingers out until the little bones inside grew long and thin. He felt the mud on each side of him and discovered that tule grass was laying there. So he took some tule and wove it around his fingers and push, push, he shoved at the darkness. It lifted a little and the plants pushed upwards with their flat leaves.

But then, bat's tule wings ripped. Still, he made enough room for himself to sit upright. So, he did. He had to hunch his back and the darkness tried to push into a ball, but bat saw some sticks lying there. So he poke, poked the sky with those sticks. That darkness lifted a little more and the plants pushed again with their flat leaves.

Now bat took some skin from his own belly and spread it between his fingers. He flap, flapped at the darkness and forced it up. Bat pushed down with his wings and it made the valleys in the mud. Flap, flap, that bat flew everywhere, shaping the land with his wings. Then he flew everywhere again, just to dry the mud out and make it hard. Bat was so tired after all his work, he slept for a week and never saw the sun coming up or the other animals crawling out of the mud. And he still doesn't see them! Because every evening as darkness comes, bat crawls out and push, push, he flaps against the sky, pushing that darkness up so that it doesn't get too heavy for us all.

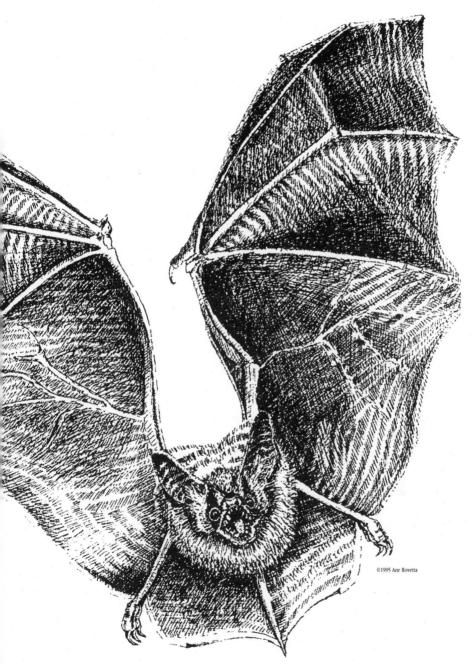

©1995 Ane Rovetta

L RANCH ROAD

DIRECTIONS: Take Highway #1 south out of Point Reyes Station. Just over the green bridge take an immediate right onto Sir Francis Drake Boulevard. Follow it out through Inverness, over the ridge and bear right onto Pierce Point Ranch Road at the fork in the road. Drive past the main entrance to Tomales Bay State Park and take a right onto L Ranch Road. Drive a few miles to the end of the road and park.

This hill above Marshall Beach is another lovely place for waiting while Luna travels her path. Walk through the gate and down the trail a ways until you see Tomales Bay below you and the eastern hills are spread out beyond. When the moon rises here all the hills glimmer in light and shadow, and the waters of the bay shine silver below. The little town of Marshall is right across the way with its fishing and sailing boats moored offshore. In dry weather this trail (which is really a continuation of an old ranch road) is traversable by jogger- stroller. No restrooms or water.

TOMALES BAY COMMUNITY PLAYGROUND

DIRECTIONS: From downtown Point Reyes Station, drive north on Highway #1 to the edge of town. About 2 blocks up the hill, on the right, you will see the tall pine trees and wrought-iron gate for the playground on the right.

An especially easy spot to reach, the playground has a very good view of the rising moon. Park in the school parking lot. Walk across the playground and through the back gate. Out on the school's grass playing field you have a wide view of Elephant Mountain and the hills above the creek to the east as the moon rises. No restrooms or water.

WHITE HOUSE POOL

• Wheelchair accessible and porta-potties • No water

DIRECTIONS: See chapter 8 "Messing About in Boats - Papermill Creek" page 115. Pull into the parking lot on the right for White House Pool Park before the road turns right.

This path borders Papermill Creek for three-quarters of a mile or so with small rest stops placed every so often that offer a clearing on the creek side with a simple bench. From here you have a unique view of the moonrise over the town of Point Reyes Station. In the foreground is the creek with Giacomini's dairy pasture spreading out flat along the flood plain. Beyond this is the backside of the dairy barns and then town itself with Elephant Mountain in the distance. The view is quite lovely.

NOTE: If you're new to moonrises be forewarned: the moon comes up very quickly. If you want the magic of waiting for the first halo of light over the hills to appear you must allow ample time to hike or drive to your viewing spot and get settled before the glorious show begins. Check the daily paper for moonrise and be at the theater well before curtain time.

©1995 Ane Rovetta

AND WHAT ABOUT THE STARS?

Of course the further you get from the lights the better your view of the stars. All the sites mentioned previously for sunsets and moonrises are ideal for seeing the stars except While House Pool, which has quite a bit of light from town to obscure the night sky.

Even if you can't stay for the complete star display you might stay long enough to spot Saturn or Jupiter or Venus, depending on the time of year - then your little ones can chant "Star light (or 'planet' light?), star bright, first star I see tonight. I wish I may, I wish I might, have this wish I wish tonight." Add a toast to the wonders of Mother Nature with a thermos of hot cocoa and you have a sensual delight.

NOTE: Watch for the bats and owls that come out at twilight. Carry flashlights.

MAYBE YOU CAN HAVE IT ALL...
THE SUN, THE MOON & THE STARS

If you are lucky enough to be here in the fall, two months of the year offer an autumnal equinox celebration not to be missed: the sun sets as the huge fall moon rises. In September and October you have a chance to feel yourself held in the balance between the light and the dark by the celestial orbs that define the cycles of life on Earth: our sun and our moon.

This fall my family watched the weather intently during the weekend scheduled for "Piper on the Ridge" on Mount Vision (see the "Calendar of Events" in the back of this book for a description). Midday proffered clear blue skies and sunshine. Late afternoon, however, saw thick cold fog roll in from the ocean. A-r-r-g-h! We reluctantly decided that it would be freezing cold up on the mountain and nobody would see a thing. So, we stayed home and built a cozy fire. Wrong. The next day the word on the street was that those who persevered were rewarded with the best moonrise and sunset ever. They had driven up the mountain to emerge into a sparkling sky above a thick blanket of fog that turned magnificent colors before dark and moonrise. Next year we'll have more faith.

TOMALES POINT TRAIL

DIRECTIONS: See Chapter #4 - "Hit the Trail!" page 60 for directions to Tomales Point Trail.

One favorite spot for viewing this seasonal benchmark from Mother Nature is the Tomales Point Trail. You must hike a good mile out from the parking area at the trail-head behind Pierce Point Ranch to come out onto the raised spine of Tomales Point. From here you have a full view in both directions: Tomales Bay and the inland hills to the east, and the western horizon where the Pacific Ocean meets the sky on your left. If the fog doesn't roll in you can see the sun slowly sink into the sea as the moon rises - more rapidly than you might expect - from the hills beyond the bay. Carry flashlights for the walk back.

©1995 Ane Rovetta

TOMALES BAY TRAIL

DIRECTIONS: Up Highway #1 from the town of Point Reyes Station about three miles north, park in the lot on the left side and take the marked trail through the stile and out towards the bay to your left.

An easy spot to reach that has a quiet, pastoral charm all its own is the end of the Tomales Bay Trail. The trail dips down past the cattle pond, then climbs up the hill and around to the right.

At the top of this promontory is a rock fire ring. Nearby is a U.S. Geological Survey marker. From this vantage point you will see the moon rise over the eastern hillside pasture which is stocked with black Angus beef cattle lowing to each other across the way. Down below you is Tomales Bay and the Inverness Ridge is right across the water, close enough to make out every *Douglas fir* and *bishop pine.* Here you can watch the sunset over the forested ridge top while the moon rises over the Point Reyes hills. This is another lovely spot for an early evening picnic. (Carry a tarp to sit on when you get out to the end. *Poison oak* is hidden low in the grasses here.)

Jogger-stroller accessible.

Owl & The Sparkles

Story & Illustration
by Ane Rovetta

O wl used to love to watch the sparkles on the surface of the ocean. He wanted to keep them all to himself. He hid them in a big bag and held on tightly to the bag. He held it so hard that his feet changed into sharp claws. He was afraid that some other animals wanted to take his sparkles, so he stayed awake guarding his "secret." Pretty soon he was so tired that he had to talk to himself to stay awake. That is when nosy Coyote heard Owl mumbling about a "secret." Coyote loves secrets. He loves to figure them out. He offered to guard Owl's secret so that Owl could go and get some sleep.

As soon as owl was gone, Coyote began shaking the secret, trying to figure out what it was. But the secret was silent. So Coyote started dancing around on top of the secret, but he couldn't feel anything with his feet. He even threw the secret around a little, but he still couldn't figure it out.

Coyote was bursting with curiosity. He started chewing on the bag until finally he chewed the top right off. He was going to open the bag just to peek at the secret.

About that time, Owl woke up and started flying back to where he left that coyote. It was late at night. Coyote opened the bag and all the sparkles flew up into the night sky. Owl watched them go. They looked so beautiful that he decided to stop coming out in the daytime. Instead he waits until night when the sky fills with the sparkling stars.

Great Blue Heron with Snake *Pacific Tree Frog, Dragonfly & Smartweed Border*
©1995 Karen Gray

Chapter 11

Picnics & Barbecues
Dining with Mother Nature

Rat....climbed up into his hole above, and after a short interval reappeared staggering under a fat, wicker luncheon-basket.

"Shove that under your feet," he observed to the Mole, as he passed it down into the boat....

"What's inside it?" asked the Mole, wriggling with curiosity.

"There's cold chicken inside it," replied the Rat briefly; "coldtonguecoldhamcoldbeefpickledgherkinssaladfrenchrollscressandwidge-spottedmeatgingerbeerlemonandsodawater---"

"O stop, stop," cried the Mole in ecstasies: "This is too much!"

"Do you really think so?" inquired the Rat seriously. "It's only what I always take on these little excursions, and the other animals are always telling me that I'm a mean beast and cut it very fine!"

Rat and Mole's Picnic – from Wind in the Willows
by Kenneth Grahame

BARBECUES

HEART'S DESIRE BEACH

• Wheelchair accessible • Restrooms • Water

DIRECTIONS: See Chapter #3 - "Where the Land Meets the Sea" page 28 for directions.

Heart's Desire Beach has barbecues with adjacent picnic tables on the right side of the beach area, sheltered from wind by the cliffs. The views from here are beautiful. Parking is only a few yards away and the restrooms include outside water faucets. The picnic area is a broad level expanse good for flying kites, playing ball and generally horsing around. The campground above Heart's Desire Beach is on a wooded promontory overlooking the bay. Under the canopy of *oak* and *bay* trees are a couple of fire rings and picnic tables with barbecues.

MILLERTON POINT

• Wheelchair accessible • Restrooms • No water

DIRECTIONS: See Chapter #3 - "Where the Land Meets the Sea" page 38 for directions.

Millerton Point, on the eastern shores of Tomales Bay, about three miles north of Point Reyes Station, has a picnic table and barbecue that look out over the cove below. This is a remarkably sheltered spot on windy days because the area faces due south and the point curves around tightly with high bluffs that are effective windbreaks. From the picnic spot it's just a hop, skip and jump down to the beach.

There is an *osprey* nest 100 feet from the picnic table for bird watching in spring and summer. Bring binoculars.

DRAKE'S BEACH
• Wheelchair accessible • Restrooms • Water

DIRECTIONS: See Chapter #3 - "Where the Land Meets the Sea" page 35 for directions.

The western side of the parking lot at Drake's Beach (to the right as you drive in) is bordered by a riparian strip of willows and shrubbery. On a grassy margin there the park maintains barbecue areas with tables. The view of the parking lot would not be my first choice but the location is the best you'll find for wind protection out on the peninsula.

On the Drake's Beach side just below the Ken Patrick Visitor Center and Drake's Beach Cafe are picnic tables sheltered from wind by the building and looking out over Drake's Bay with a view of the bluffs over Limantour Beach.

©1995 Ane Rovetta

PICNIC TABLES ONLY

For simple picnics with no cooking there are some places in Point Reyes that will get you off the ground in damp weather. Behind the **BEAR VALLEY VISITOR CENTER** are a couple of picnic tables that are sheltered from cars and wind and that have lovely views of the horse pasture above. **THE MORGAN HORSE RANCH** has a picnic table sheltered from wind just opposite the training ring and tack barn. Porta-potty nearby.

    FIVE BROOKS STABLES has picnic tables in three spots: at the top of the hill above the stables, at the edge of the old Mill Pond above the stables, and between the stables and corrals down below. This last site has four or five tables and is well sheltered from wind. There is an old weathered hay wagon parked here for children to play around. Porta-potties. No water.

    THE INVERNESS LIBRARY AND JACK MASON MUSEUM has a picnic table under the tree in the side garden that opens onto the street. A Porta-potty is in the back.

    THE TOMALES BAY COMMUNITY PLAYGROUND on Highway #1 just north of Point Reyes Station has a picnic table under the pine trees in the playground. No restrooms. No water.

    THE TOMALES BAY OYSTER COMPANY provides a few picnic tables overlooking the bay for its customers. A soda machine and porta-potties are on-site. A lovely place for a warm afternoon or evening.

    THE HOG ISLAND OYSTER COMPANY provides a few picnic tables and barbecues for its customers. Right on the edge of Tomales Bay, this is a beautiful spot on a sunny day.

    THE ROUGE ET NOIRE CHEESE FACTORY in Hick's Valley has many picnic tables situated in grassy landscaped grounds, a few scattered around the lovely duck pond, and a few that are wheelchair accessible right off the parking area under trellises. The idea is that you buy their cheese and goodies for a repast on the grounds, but nobody ever complains if you bring your own picnic basket as well. (They do sell beer and fine wines to accompany your picnic as well as sandwiches, breads, coffee, teas, cookies and some fresh fruit.)

    PIERCE POINT RANCH has a picnic table set in the ranch compound with a beautiful view across the fields to the hills in the south. Handicapped accessible.

PLANT PARK in Inverness has a few picnic tables. It's a level spot in the alder trees just above the parking area for the Inverness post office and pizza parlor.

©1995 Ane Rovetta

Turkey Vultures
The Soaring Untouchables
Story by Jules Evens

A fter the highest tides of each month, my six year old son, Noah, and I like to walk the beach on the Point Reyes Peninsula, north of San Francisco, and comb the wrack for whatever treasures have washed in. Sometimes we find glass flotation bulbs from Japanese fishing nets, empty Russian vodka flasks, carcasses of strange fish, or smooth, bleached bones, beautifully weathered. The bulbs and bottles embossed with foreign characters we collect to place on the window sill. We marvel over the fish - an eerily primitive sturgeon, a bat ray with its nearly human face - but always from a slight distance. The bones we gather: the hollow wing bone of a shearwater makes a fine penny whistle.

We are not the only scavengers to comb the beach. There are tracks of others. The deliberate trail of a striped skunk parallels the highest tide line, as if he was worried about getting his feet wet. The sharp impressions of a gray fox's paws weave through the seaweed debris, and webbed tracks of gulls and forked tracks of ravens surround the bird carcasses. But the first to find beach-cast carrion are the vultures. The harbinger of something dead out there is the flurry of vultures several hundred yards down the beach.

Turkey Vultures, commonly known as buzzards, are among the most common large soaring birds in the skies of North America. Even from a great distance, they are easy to identify. While soaring, they tip, or rock, from side to side, ever adjusting their flight feathers to the changing air currents. This flight pattern has earned them the nick-name "tippy-gliders" by children. The conspicuous separation of their long, primary feathers causes the outer tip of the wings to appear slotted. Other large soaring birds - eagles and hawks - hold their wings on a horizontal plane as they soar. Vultures tilt their wings skyward, forming a shallow V-shape.

Their pattern of coloration is distinctive. The underside of the vulture body and forward portion of the wing are charcoal black, contrasting sharply with the silver trailing part of the wing. Ospreys, most red tailed hawks and other buteos have light-colored underparts.

Among diurnal birds of prey, turkey vultures are the most primitive family. They belong to the genus *Cathartes* from the Greek root meaning "purifier," a name that aptly describes their janitorial niche in the environment. They assume no pretense. Like the Hindu caste the Untouchables, vultures keep to themselves - deferential to others, modest and self-effacing. Evolution has cast them in a degenerate mold, not of character, but of physical prowess. Their talons, weapons of death in other birds of prey, are too weak to grasp or kill their prey. Their jaw musculature is also weak and their beaks are ill-suited for tearing tendons and flesh. So, they are consigned to the lesser task of cleaning-up the left overs.

Other North American birds that qualify as scavengers - crows, ravens, magpies, jays, and even eagles - are generalists, omnivores, capable of exploiting a wide variety of foods. Turkey Vultures are specialists - "obligate carrion eaters" - narrowly-adapted to eating only dead animals. Evolution has compensated for their handicap by providing them with an uncanny ability to find dead things.

Two attributes in particular - acute smell and an incredible lightness of being - work in concert to account for the Turkey Vulture's carcass-finding expertise. Their sense of smell - poorly-developed in most other species of birds - allows them to use odor as a cue for finding food. They can locate even small- and medium-sized carcasses, like rodents, snakes and rabbits, before other scavengers find them. Vultures seem to prefer freshly killed carcasses to older putrefied ones, though this may be an artifact of their keen ability to locate carcasses quickly.

Their remarkable aerodynamics, a function of small body size relative to the large surface area of their out-stretched wings, expressed as "wing-load," allows them to sail down closer to the ground where they can best use their sense of smell.

The real measure of success for any species is survival. Turkey vultures, or creatures very much like them, have been riding thermals over North America since the early Eocene, for perhaps 65 million years. They range across the Americas farther north or south than any other member of their family, from the northern United States to the southern tip of South America. They survived and even benefited from several mass die-offs, including the great Pleistocene extinctions. More recently, America's love affair with the automobile has provided the ever-vigilant vulture with a new and expanding resource - road kill.

TURKEY VULTURE IDENTIFICATION

Turkey Vultures are easy to identify even from a great distance. Among North American birds of prey, their six-foot wingspan is surpassed only by the Bald and Golden eagles. While soaring they tend to tip, or rock, from side to side, ever adjusting their flight feathers to the changing air currents. Other large soaring birds - eagles and hawks - tend to hold their wings on a horizontal plane. TVs tilt their wings skyward, in profile forming a shallow V-shape ("dihedral"). Turkey Vultures do not fan or flex their tails as do other common soaring Buteos like the Red-tailed or Broad-winged Hawk. Also, when soaring, the long primary feathers are conspicuously separated, causing the outer tip of the wings to appear slotted. The vulture has a tiny head, whereas other birds of prey are bulky-headed.

Their pattern of coloration is also distinctive. In turkey vultures, the underside of the body and the forward portion of the wing are charcoal black, contrasting sharply with the silvery flight feathers, the trailing portion of the wing. Black Vultures have white patches out toward the wing-tips and a much heavier flight. Ospreys, most Red-tails and other buteos have light-colored underparts. Most eagles are dark underneath, but lack the silvery flight feathers and have more rectangular wings rather than the more pointed, sail shaped wing of the vulture.

The vultures gather in small groups, taking turns at the roadside deer diner. I always wonder why we rarely see a road-killed vulture.

Every morning, turkey vultures are roosted atop the bare alders in the dry creek bed below my house: a dozen huge birds facing east, wings outstretced or akimbo, their black plumage steaming, drying in the first rays of the sun. Posed still and silent they seem mythical, as though they are performing some occult ritual, or praying. They gathered at this night roost yesterday, or a million years ago, waiting for the next morning's convection currents to carry them aloft in their endless search for a fresh beach-cast seal or a stillborn fawn. Today they are apt to find a sheep carcass abandoned by coyotes at dawn, or a road-killed raccoon.

The roost is close enough so that through binoculars I can see their blood red, naked heads, the wrinkled, sagging jowls, and the wide-eyed stare that lends them each a kind of cautious and vulnerable expression. Their baldheadedness has not endeared them to humans, but it contributes to their success as scavengers. As they probe the eyes or alimentary canal of a decaying carcass, the offal may adhere to their skin, but there are no feathers in which the attendant bacteria can proliferate. Soon after eating the vultures head will be dry cleaned by the air and sun, neutralizing the potential for disease.

While turkey vultures tend to gather in large flocks to forage and roost, they retire in solitude to breed. In 20 years of hiking the arroyos and canyons of the American West, only once have I stumbled on a vulture nest. It was located in the hollow heart of a fallen fir. The adult was absent, and the two chicks, snow white in downy dress, hunkered down in their dark hide-out and hissed, cat-like, at me. Vultures lack a voice box (syrinx), so are functionally mute, but when threatened they utter an inhalant "hiss," described by Victorian ornithologist Elliot Coues as the "seething noise of a hot iron plunged in water."

On one of our recent beach walks, Noah and I noticed a small flock of vultures flush several hundred yards down the beach. There was an onshore breeze and four vultures took flight easily, three or four flaps and they were aloft, circling on fixed wings. As we approached the oddly shaped prey which lay on the beach, my heart quickened. It seemed about the size of a small person lying on his side. I told my son to stop and wait. I walked ahead cautiously, like a dog approaching a carcass that it's not sure is dead. I was relieved, but not much, when I got close enough to see that it was not a human being, but a turtle being – a large sea turtle, a Leatherback. His carapace was about five feet in length. He was staring blindly shoreward. His eyes were gone, probably the food of the vultures overhead.

I called Noah to come see this marvelous creature.

We would have wanted to take home a turtle skull, or one of the polygonal bones imbedded in the carapace. Each contains such strange symmetry and purpose, such functional beauty. But the carcass was too fresh. The creature was too close to life and suffering, too recently alive, for us to render its body for our curiosity or souvenirs. We could still see the graceful trail in the sand where the turtle had crawled up the beach. The rhythm of the arcs in the sand reminded us of the snow angels we make in the Sierras every winter by lying in the fresh fallen snow and flapping our arms. Unlike the bones and feathers of the winter beach, the turtle's body had not yet done penance under the sun, been weathered by wind and waves, or purified by the shy band of vultures that circled, still, overhead.

They spend so much time ranging over the landscape, looking down on us. All things are connected, having passed through the clear vision of this bird.

Our knees were damp from kneeling by the turtle's side. Noah and I stood up and continued down the beach, leaving the tide, the turtle and the vultures to their unfinished business.

- for Harrowsmith's Country Life - " Wild Lives"
September 7, 1990

FIELD NOTES

FIELD NOTES

Turkey Vulture with Bull Tule Elk Grazing *Wild Oats Border*
©1995 Karen Gray

Chapter 12

Horseback Riding & Llama Trekking in the Park

FIVE BROOKS STABLES

Five Brooks Stables is the horseback riding concession for the Point Reyes National Seashore. They rent horses for guided rides on an hourly, half-day or full-day basis. Kids usually need to be eight years old or older before they can go out. There are a number of trails for horses that take off from the Five Brooks Trailhead and lead up into the *bishop pine* forest and the meadows on the Inverness Ridge.

The stables also do hay rides by arrangement. They have a big western wagon with large Belgian horses that pull in harness. The ride is a thrilling one for children, a perfect occasion for singing and shouting. Special rides out to Wildcat Camp over the Pacific can be arranged and include an overnight camp out. Five Brooks Stables telephone is (415) 663-1570.

Many people trailer their own horses out to Point Reyes. Both Bear Valley Trailhead and Limantour Beach have ample parking for

©1995 Ane Rovetta

trucks and trailers. Riders take off down the beaches or up the trails from here.

If some in your family are too young to ride or if horseback is not your choice, what about HIKING WITH LLAMAS? Camelid Capers offers short hikes and long hikes with these endearing creatures - the ones with the unnaturally long eyelashes and petite paws. They will carry all your picnic supplies and gear while your party walks along in ease. Originally from South America, the llama is especially adept at steep terrain and heavy loads. They are a welcome sight in the High Sierra and Point Reyes where trail erosion is a serious concern. The soft pads they have instead of hooves are much less destructive than our traditional beasts of burden. Plus, they are adorable! Camelid Capers can be reached at (415) 663-9371.

©1995 Ane Rovetta

FIELD NOTES

Father and Child Seen Through Window of Library *Wildflower Border*
©1995 Karen Gray

Chapter 13

Libraries & Bookstores

INVERNESS PUBLIC LIBRARY

• Wheelchair accessible

DIRECTIONS: Go south on Highway #1 over the green bridge from downtown Point Reyes Station. Take an immediate right onto Sir Francis Drake Boulevard. Follow Sir Francis Drake to the village of Inverness. Take the second left turn onto the second marked "Inverness Way" (at the Inverness Inn). The library is the pale-yellow Victorian on your right just one block up at the corner of Park Place.

This is a part-time library supported by dedicated volunteers from the Inverness community. It is a good place to go for a quiet read or to research a particular question about the Point Reyes area. Because the Jack Mason Museum is adjacent, there is a wealth of information here about local history. Call for hours (415) 669-1288. Part of the county-wide system.

©1995 Ane Rovetta

POINT REYES PUBLIC LIBRARY

This is also a branch of our county-wide library system. If you have a Marin County Library card you can check books out of this library while you are visiting here and return them to your neighborhood branch library when you return home. The Point Reyes Library is especially friendly for children, with bean bag chairs and an alcove in which little people can read or be read to. Of course anybody can read and do research in the library. The hours are part-time with some evenings open as well as daytime.

The Point Reyes Library is near the corner of Highway #1 and 4th Street in the strip of businesses that includes the West Marin Pharmacy and Joe's Diner. Call ahead for hours (415) 663-8375.

BEAR VALLEY VISITOR CENTER BOOKSTORE

DIRECTIONS: Head south on Highway #1 from Point Reyes Station. Take a right onto Sir Francis Drake Boulevard just over the green bridge. Take the first left onto Bear Valley Road. (Caution! This is a blind curve.) In one-and-a-half miles you will see the sign for the drive to the visitor center on your right - it is the large barn structure at the end.

This is the largest bookstore of the three in the National Seashore. It carries specific guides to the Point Reyes area as well as more generic texts on flora and fauna, books about marine mammals (especially the gray whale), wilderness experience, native American peoples, and local history. All the books are affordable quality paperbacks. A good selection of maps, posters, postcards and note cards are also in stock. This is the place to go for free information on the seashore as well: the quarterly newspaper with schedule of events, the color brochure outlining the park and its highlights, the coded hiking trail map and detailed handouts on specific animals or natural events.

The visitor center is open 7 days a week from 9 to 5 every day of the year, except Christmas Day. Call for information (415) 663-1092.

KEN PATRICK VISITOR CENTER BOOKSTORE

DIRECTIONS: The visitor center is on Drake's Bay. Follow Highway #1 south out of Point Reyes Station. Just past the green bridge take a right onto Sir Francis Drake Boulevard. Go through the village of Inverness and over the hill. Bear left when the road forks, staying on Sir Francis Drake. About 7 miles out you will see the sign for Drake's Bay and the symbol for food. Take this left down to the bay and park. Ken Patrick Visitor Center is open just part-time.

The visitor center has the same kinds of books here as are at Bear Valley Visitor Center. It's just a much smaller selection. Call for information (415) 669-1250.

©1996 Ane Rovetta

POINT REYES LIGHTHOUSE VISITOR CENTER BOOKSTORE

DIRECTIONS: Same as for the Ken Patrick Visitor Center above only go past the Drake's Bay turn off and follow Sir Francis Drake Boulevard all the way out to the end. Park and walk the quarter-mile to the visitor center.

The lighthouse bookstore stocks a full selection of books on the gray whale and lighthouse history. Because this is a famously good point for viewing the whale migration the whole visitor center explores this theme. Posters, cards, postcards and guides are sold. Call ahead for hours and weather information (415) 669-1534.

BROWN STUDY BOOKS

This bookstore is on Main Street in Point Reyes right across from the super market. It carries new and used books, paperbacks and hardbound. There are easy chairs set in a lounging area for relaxing while you read. A special children's section low to the ground with small chairs welcomes children to browse and read in the study area. Parents are also invited to read aloud to their children here. Call for information (415) 663-1633.

POINT REYES BOOKS

This bookstore is on Main Street (Highway #1) in Point Reyes Station, right across from the post office. It carries new books in hardbound and paperback. Some cards and postcards. Call for information (415) 663-1303.

FIELD NOTES

Scarecrow with Crow *Pea Vine Border*
©1995 Karen Gray

Chapter 14

Local Medical Care

Residents and visitors to West Marin are fortunate to have high quality medical care available seven days a week. All practices take "call" and home visits are common. Physicians, nurse practitioners, midwives and paramedics play vital roles in providing care for all those in need, including hospital admission, if necessary.

West Marin Medical Center: Dr. Michael Whitt has operated this general practice since around 1966. Both Dr. Whitt and a nurse practitioner see patients on a regular basis at the center. (Dr. Whitt is a writer whose poems and journals are published locally, most recently in the literary quarterly "Estero.")

The practice is open Monday through Friday and Saturday mornings. Phone (415) 663-1082. Located at #11150 Highway #1 - the main street in Point Reyes Station - just east of the Station House Cafe.

Coastal Health Alliance: Point Reyes Station, Stinson Beach, and Bolinas. Dr. Michael Witte is the Medical Director of these clinics. Many of the staff, including

Dr. Witte, are fluent in Spanish. Physicians and nurse practitioner/midwives provide care at the clinics.

The Point Reyes Medical Clinic is open Monday through Friday and on weekends. Phone (415) 663-8666. Located at #3 6th Street (across the street from the Dance Palace and Papermill Creek Children's Corner).

The Bolinas Family Practice is open Monday through Friday (415) 868-0124. Located at #7 Wharf Road, the main street in Bolinas.

The Stinson Beach Medical Center is open four half-days a week; telephone (415) 868-9656. Located at #3419 Coast Highway #1, the main street in Stinson Beach; at the south end of town near the Claudia Chapline Gallery.

PARAMEDICS

Paramedics are available by calling the universal emergency number 911. They are highly trained members of the Marin County Fire Department stationed, 24 hours-a-day, at the Firehouse in Point Reyes Station. Their medical ambulance is state-of-the-art and allows them to be in contact with advising doctors at the admitting hospital while in transit. Located at the corner of 3rd and "C" Streets.

FIELD NOTES

Mother and Child Watching Raccoon in Campground *Pine Cone Border*
©1995 Karen Gray

Chapter 15

Planned Field Trips & Campouts

• **AUDUBON CANYON RANCH** • #4900 Highway #1, Stinson Beach, CA 94970, (415) 868-9244. Ranch open to the public some months, docents-in-the-schools program, guided tours of the ranch. Museum, book store, membership and newsletter available.

• **CAMELID CAPERS - LLAMMA TREKKING** • Point Reyes, CA, 94956 (415) 663-9371. (Call and leave your name and address. They will mail information to you.)

• **FOOTLOOSE FORAYS WITH MICHAEL ELLIS** • Post Office Box #175, Sebastapol, CA 95473, (707) 829-1844. Guided educational field trips: local and around the world, one day to two weeks. Some for adults, others for the entire family.

• **MARIN COUNTY NATURALIST FIELD WALKS WITH BOB STEWART** • Marin County Open Space District, Civic Center - Room #417, San Rafael, CA 94903, (415) 499-3647. Call to be on the mailing list and receive the bi-monthly schedule of walks ((10-12 each month) all over the county. Some are wheelchair accessible and provide assistive listening devices by prior arrangement.

• **MARINE MAMMAL CENTER** • Fort Cronkite, Golden Gate National Recreation Area, Sausalito, CA 94932, (415) 289-7325. Injured mammal rescue, rehabilitation and release into the wild. Some public tours, membership and written information available.

• **POINT REYES BIRD OBSERVATORY** • #4990 Shoreline Highway, Stinson Beach, CA 94970, (415) 868-1221. Palo Marin Field Station open to the public for displays and bird-banding demonstrations. Membership, quarterly newsletter and many publications available.

• **POINT REYES FIELD SEMINARS** • Point Reyes National Seashore, Point Reyes Station, CA 94956, (415) 663-1200. Field seminars available on the natural world of Point Reyes, birds of Point Reyes, especially for educators, photography, arts and natural crafts, and field trips especially for families. Some half-day, some day-long, some week-long. Call for quarterly catalog of classes and fees to be mailed to you.

• **POINT REYES NATIONAL SEASHORE HEADQUARTERS** • Point Reyes National Seashore, Point Reyes, CA 94956, (415) 663-1092. Call for campground reservations, information on free ranger talks, walks and trips, and general park information. Clem Miller Environmental Education Center workshops and events (415) 663-1920. Will mail quarterly newsletter ("Seashore Events and Information") on request. Bear Valley information line provides recorded hours, weather, and an events update on the telephone message (adapted for the deaf) at (415) 663-9029. Seashore administrative offices (415) 663-8522. Point Reyes Field Seminars (415) 663-1200 (see listing above).

• **POINT REYES YOUTH HOSTEL** • Point Reyes Station, CA 94956, (415) 663-8811. Member of the American Youth Hostel Association. Located on side road off Limantour Road, just opposite Muddy Hollow turn-off, about half-a-mile from Limantour Beach. Men and women's dormitory sleeping with bunks, family accomodations, shared kitchen, nominal fees. Limited wheelchair access. Call for information and reservations between 7:30 and 9:30 a.m., or 4:30 and 9:30 p.m.

- **SAMUEL P. TAYLOR STATE PARK** • Ranger Station, Lagunitas, CA 94950, (415) 488-9897. Call for general information and salmon run updates in the fall. Day use and overnight facilities. Group and wheelchair accessible campsites. Dogs on leash allowed. For camping reservations call: MISTIX 1-800-444-7275.

- **TAMALSAKA KAYAK AND CANOE RENTALS AND INSTRUCTION** • 19225 Highway #1, Marshall, CA 94940, (415) 663-1743. Call for schedule of classes and outings on Tomales Bay, Drake's Bay, Bolinas Lagoon, Estero Americano.

- **TRAILHEAD RENTALS** • Olema, CA 94950, (415) 663-1958. At the intersection of Highway #1 and Bear Valley Road (next to the Bear Valley Inn) in Olema. Call ahead for hours and availability - binoculars, bicycles, helmets, kites, children's seats.

- **TOMALES BAY STATE PARK RANGER STATION** • Inverness, CA 94937, (415) 669-1140. Bayside beaches, camp grounds, picnic grounds. Call ahead for overnight reservations.

- **WILD CARE TERWILLIGER NATURE EDUCATION CENTER AND WILDLIFE REHABILITATION** • Post Office Box #150930, San Rafael, CA 94915, (415) 453-1000. School programs, public programs, wildlife hospital, field trips. Membership, volunteer corps, and newsletter. Call ahead for visits.

Yearly Calendar of Events for Children

JANUARY

Gray whales migrating south (peaks early in month)
Sea lions and elephant seals at Chimney Rock and outer headlands
Mushrooms begin to emerge (check Point Reyes Field Seminars for study)
Very low minus tides for tide-pooling
High tides for kayaking and wildlife observation
Storms at sea - good beach combing
Point Reyes Bird Observatory winter banding
Allen's hummingbirds return to the area (late in month)
Oranges come into Toby's Feed Barn

NOTE: Be cautious on the beaches and cliffs this time of year. Sneaker waves can catch you off guard and the tides move in quickly enough to leave you stranded. Always carry your tidebook and wristwatch.

FEBRUARY

Purple Douglas iris and other wildflowers begin to bloom at Chimney Rock,
    Kehoe Beach bluffs, Tomales Bay Trail, Point Reyes-Petaluma Road
    around Nicasio Reservoir
Wild currants burst into bright pink bloom, attracting hummingbirds
Extreme minus tides and high tides
Aquatic newts migrating with winter rains from woodland to ponds and
    streams for mating: Hagmaier's pond, Bear Valley creek
Pacific tree frogs and red-legged frogs coming out of hibernation in mud to
    sing at pond's edge

MARCH

VERNAL EQUINOX: day and night are equal
Windiest month of the year
Ospreys return to their traditional nests on Inverness Ridge and Tomales Bay
Spring wildflower bloom peaks at Kehoe beach bluffs, Chimney Rock,
        Tomales Bay Trail, Point Reyes-Petaluma Road around Nicasio
        Reservoir
Gray whales migrating north - mothers and calves move close to shore
Audubon Canyon Ranch opens mid-month
Pussy willows along creeksides and marshes bloom
Morgan Horse Ranch Day in Bear Valley, Point Reyes National Seashore

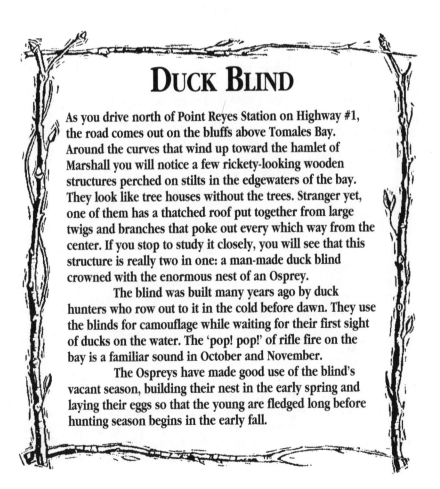

DUCK BLIND

As you drive north of Point Reyes Station on Highway #1, the road comes out on the bluffs above Tomales Bay. Around the curves that wind up toward the hamlet of Marshall you will notice a few rickety-looking wooden structures perched on stilts in the edgewaters of the bay. They look like tree houses without the trees. Stranger yet, one of them has a thatched roof put together from large twigs and branches that poke out every which way from the center. If you stop to study it closely, you will see that this structure is really two in one: a man-made duck blind crowned with the enormous nest of an Osprey.

    The blind was built many years ago by duck hunters who row out to it in the cold before dawn. They use the blinds for camouflage while waiting for their first sight of ducks on the water. The 'pop! pop!' of rifle fire on the bay is a familiar sound in October and November.

    The Ospreys have made good use of the blind's vacant season, building their nest in the early spring and laying their eggs so that the young are fledged long before hunting season begins in the early fall.

APRIL

Bird banding at Point Reyes Bird Observatory
Barn swallows and many other species begin building their nests
Strawberry Festival at Kule Loklo Indian Village
Chimney Rock and Kehoe bluffs full wildflower display continues
Sea birds begin nesting on sea stacks at Chimney Rock: gulls, murres,
         guillemots, cormorants
Baby chicks, ducklings and rabbits for sale at Toby's Feed Barn
Old Pacific dogwood blooms across the creek on Bear Valley Trail
Gray whales migrating north
Foals and mares come out into the pasture at Stewart Ranch in Olema

MAY

Brown pelicans arrive from nesting grounds in Baja
Velellas ("by-the-wind sailors" jellyfish) wash up onto the beaches
Yellow and lavender bush lupine blooms
Red-tailed hawks fledge from nests (lots of commotion in the tree tops)
Salmonberry is ripe; native blackberry begins to ripen
Rattlesnake grass heads are full along the roadsides

JUNE

SUMMER SOLSTICE - longest day of the year
Buckeye ("horse chestnut") trees in full bloom
Ripe cherries come into Toby's Feed Barn
Osprey young fledge from nests
Watch for ducklings in Muddy Hollow Pond and Limantour Estero
Many new fawns out in the meadows in Bear Valley
Western Weekend and 4-H Livestock Show in Point Reyes Station
         (first weekend in June)

NOTE: You haven't seen anything yet if you've never seen show chickens! Fancy leggings of colorful feathers and exaggerated combs and wattles await your astonished viewing. The patterning on their feathers can be wonderfully intricate. These animals are fascinating. The same goes for the wide variety of rabbits - from lop-eared to cotton-tail, long-haired to short, they are fetching creatures.

4-H JUNIOR LIVESTOCK SHOW

4-H has been a part of growing up in Point Reyes since the 1920s. Most of the kids involved are from the ranching community, of course, but some town kids also participate from year to year, learning to raise and care for smaller animals. During Western Weekend in June our local 4-H puts on the Junior Livestock Show at the Red Barn in Point Reyes Station.

Kids trailer their larger animals in from the outlying ranches at dawn on Saturday. Youngsters are out in their rubber boots with soap, hair conditioner, hoses, brushes, hair dryers and bootblack to groom their animals to a shine for judging.

Dairy cows, calves, sheep, goats, horses, rabbits and chickens are all on show in their stalls (sometimes piglets, too). During the day, children enter their animals into competition by breed, age and class. Coveted blue ribbons and trophies are awarded.

The animals are left with their awards on display for viewing throughout the day. The proud owners who raised them are around to answer questions and sometimes to take offers for sale. The sights, smells and sounds of this many animals is a thrill for kids. Most animals are docile enough for your children to approach with permission from the owners.

JULY

Big Time celebration at Kule Loklo - a re-created Coast Miwok Village
Fresh corn and watermelons arrive at Toby's Feed Barn
Audubon Canyon Ranch closes to the public
Sonoma County Fair: Livestock Show & Rodeo at
       Santa Rosa Fairgrounds
Summerstock Players Children's Theater at Dance Palace
Blackberries ripen

MOW OUR WEEDS
& LEAVE THE BLACKBERRIES

The blackberries along the highways and byways of western Marin are free of toxic pesticides and herbicides. We have a local heroine, Donna Sheehan, to thank for this. An artist living in Marshall (a community that grew up on the narrow fringe between the coast highway and the shores of Tomales Bay), Donna and her neighbors picked blackberries in late summer as an annual tradition. Blackberry picking was part of what made summer summer.

Then the California Department of Transportation began using chemical weed killers along the roadsides to kill all the vegetation with a hose from the back of a truck. Donna and her outraged friends banded together to form *MOW: Mow Our Weeds!*

They wanted the road crews to mow the weeds and leave the blackberry thickets the way they always had. Nobody wanted to eat blackberries sprayed with poison. It was a fight that took demonstrations, lawsuits, and tenacity over a number of years, but eventually Donna and her neighbors won out: no more poisons on our blackberries.

So, if you pull your car over some late summer day to celebrate Mother Nature's gifts to us all, remember our local heroine.

AUGUST

Full harvest moon rises over Elephant Mountain in the evening

Coast live oak acorns begin to ripen: acorn woodpeckers go to work storing them in Douglas fir tree trunks (granaries) for winter

Scrub Jays are busy burying acorns in the ground for winter (the ones they forget about sprout into new oak trees)

Sea lavender blooms at tidelands on Millerton Point, Limantour Marsh, Shield's Marsh and Drake's Bay

Grasshoppers are out in the dry grasslands

Pickleweed turns bright fall colors at tide line

West Marin Music Festival with Children's Chorus productions

Meteor showers - August 15th or so: the Leonids

SEPTEMBER

AUTUMNAL EQUINOX: day and night are equal
Hunter's moon rises in the evening over Elephant Mountain
Elephant (Black) Mountain Hike: Organized hike up the back
    side of the mountain to view the area as full moon rises and sun sets
    into the Pacific (Check local paper for details)
Now through October is our 'Indian Summer' - days are hot and Tomales
    Bay is warmest for swimming
Sand Castle Contest on Drake's Beach (weekend after Labor Day or Labor Day
    weekend)
Big leaf maples turn gold
Poison oak turns beautiful fall colors - don't touch!
Wintering birds return - good time to visit the estuaries (Abbott's lagoon,
    Limantour Estero, Bolinas Lagoon)
National Coast Cleanup Day - Call Point Reyes Lighthouse for details
    (669-1534)

PIPER ON THE RIDGE

Some years ago an Inverness person especially attuned to the beauties of Point Reyes, Kate Munger, originated a local tradition called "Piper on the Ridge." She found a gifted bagpiper, in his kilt, who comes every year to play his pipes to the setting sun as he strolls the grassy hilltop of Mount Vision. People bring their blankets to spread on the grass and their evening picnics to enjoy an hour or two before the sun goes down. As the piper plays, his lilting tunes float out across the hillsides. When the sun disappears behind the fog bank out at sea, everyone climbs to the crest of the hill and watches for the moon to rise over the eastern hills.

Kate decided that she would give the event to the Environmental Action Committee, our local environmental watchdog organization. Being a nonprofit dependent on donations, it was the perfect new steward for the event because an essential part of the Piper on the Ridge is that everyone who comes has to pay the piper! So, your family can share a community picnic (bring your own), glory in the gifts of Mother Nature's seasons and support the Environmental Action Committee - all in the same evening.

OCTOBER

Hunter's moon rises in the evening over Elephant Mountain
Papermill Creek Children's Corner and Point Reyes Pre-School Halloween
        Carnival - check local paper for details or call PMCCC 663-9114)
Local apiarists harvest and sell their honey
Pumpkins come into Toby's Feed Barn
Gravenstein apples harvested in Sonoma County (early in month)
Dawn redwood in Bear Valley Creek turns red

HALLOWEEN CARNIVAL

The preschool Halloween Carnival is great fun for younger children. Parents from the Papermill Creek Children's Corner and the Point Reyes Pre-School work for weeks in preparation for the event held in Toby's Feed Barn or the Red Barn the Sunday before Halloween.

Local children dress in their costumes and come out in the afternoon to shriek through the haunted house, hide in the huge pumpkin, try their luck at the harvest barrel, ride ponies, and do the cake walk. The stalls are set up with walls of hay bales and the whole place is decorated with pumpkins and sheaves of corn.

For adults, barbecued local oysters, beer and a silent auction of local treasures are offered all afternoon. The event is worth coming out for just to see the parade of tiny fairies, bumblebees, gypsies, pirates, goblins and witches.

NOVEMBER

First frosts usually begin - "Frost on the Pumpkin"
Hawks migrate into the coastal region
First rains bring steelhead and salmon migrating up Papermill and Lagunitas
        Creeks to spawn (call Samuel P. Taylor State Park for information:
        415/488-9897)
Brown pelicans start to head south (white pelicans winter here)
Bird banding at PRBO ends
Migratory waterfowl numbers peak this month and next in Point Reyes:
        good time to visit Abbott's Lagoon, Limantour Estero, and Bolinas
        Lagoon
Gray whales begin migrating around Point Reyes

DECEMBER

WINTER SOLSTICE - shortest day of the year
Herring run in Tomales Bay if heavy rains occur this month
Dance Palace Christmas Crafts Fair
Extreme minus tides begin for tide pooling/high tides for kayaking
Live nativity and Christmas Carols at Toby's Feed Barn (check local paper)
Gray whales migrating south - peak late in month

PAPERMILL CREEK CHILDREN'S CORNER
TREE SALE

Every year Chris Giacomini of Toby's Feed Barn puts on the Papermill Creek Children's Corner Christmas Tree Sale. For two weeks before Christmas, the garden yard at Toby's is stocked with cut fresh *noble* and *Douglas firs*, all reasonably priced. Locals and weekenders out for the holidays buy their trees here to benefit the preschool.

If you can combine your tree selection with the day of carols and nativity you are in for a real treat. Each year a local couple with a newborn is asked to act in the "tableau vivant" of the nativity. It can only last an hour or two since standing still with an infant in the feed barn takes a concerted effort. A donkey and a few sheep are usually brought in to complete the scene set among the hay bales. Grown ups and children sit on the stacked bales opposite and sing carols together. Egg nog, apple cider and cookies are for sale to benefit Halleck Creek Riding Club. Toby's is right in the middle of Point Reyes Station on Main Street.

WHAT TO DO ON A RAINY DAY

The Point Reyes area has wonderful things to offer on a rainy day. If it's really storming, of course, you will need to be inside. Here are some suggestions:

THE BEAR VALLEY VISITOR CENTER is beautifully designed for children and adults to experience the wonder of Point Reyes without being out in it. The large barn structure houses many displays that you can explore. Beautifully designed **dioramas** depict native *flora and fauna* in their natural habitat – *harbor seals, deer, badger, fox, skunk, bobcat*, and many birds. (Look up! See the *eagle, ravens, woodpeckers* and others flying overhead.) Steps lead up to a "promontory" equipped with a **telescope** that you can manipulate for spotting the animals in the displays down below, just as you would in the wild. A **touch table** filled with *bones, whale baleen, antler, fur* and other objects from nature is there for the children to explore. A **seismograph** that works around the clock is on display with elaborate maps and explanatory notes for older children. A **documentary film** about Point Reyes runs for about 12 minutes. It explains the history of the seashore and explores its beauty and diversity. Best of all, **rangers** trained in nature interpretation are available here to answer your questions. A good-sized book selection of guides and naturalist writings is for sale, as well as posters and cards.

The award-winning architecture is especially inviting on rainy days. The walls are warm redwood and there is a cozy area of comfortable couches around the woodstove that the rangers keep burning on cold days. The view out to the horse pasture is beautiful.

THE KEN PATRICK VISITOR CENTER and **DRAKE'S BEACH CAFÉ** are a winning combination on a rainy day. (The Visitor Center hours change, so call ahead 415/669-1250). Sometimes, if it is really stormy the café closes. However, it is usually open 7 days a week from 10am to 6pm. The Visitor Center is well designed for leisurely exploration with a cozy area of couches in front of expansive windows that look out onto Drake's Bay and the cliffs above. You could sit here quietly and read for hours. A *pelican* is hung just overhead for easy viewing. A *great blue heron* sits on the counter. The skeleton of a *minke whale* is suspended in the center. An excellent small exhibit of Coast Miwok Indian basketry, clothing and tools is here. A carefully designed display of the trade routes and cargo of the ships from the

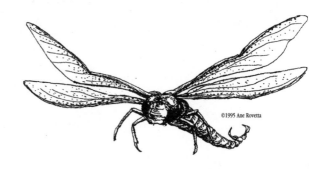

©1995 Ane Rovetta

173

time of Sir Francis Drake adorns the back wall. Especially fascinating is the large salt water aquarium stocked with natives from the inter-tidal zone of Point Reyes: *anemones, sea stars crab, eels, mussels, barnacles* and assorted fish. Interpretive rangers are on staff here, ready to answer your questions. A selection of books on Sir Francis Drake, Point Reyes and the gray whale are for sale, as well as some posters and cards.

DRAKE'S BEACH CAFÉ is just next door. A crackling fire in the woodstove gives a welcome feeling to the place as you enter. One whole wall is large picture windows overlooking the beach and the bay - a dramatic view when the surf is up. The café is a local favorite for weekend breakfast. The lunch menu includes seafood, salads, burgers and homemade tamales. Oyster stew or clam chowder are usually on the menu, too. An antique telescope with a step-stool is focused on the ocean for children to enjoy. If the rain lets up you can always run out on the beach to see what treasures the storm waves have washed up.

THE MARIN MUSEUM OF THE AMERICAN INDIAN is just west of Novato on Novato Boulevard. It houses a gallery of baskets, tools, and other artifacts in attractive displays. There is a gift shop. The Museum is open Tuesday through Saturday from 10 am to 4 pm and Sunday from Noon to 4 pm. (415) 897-4064.

THE ROUGE ET NOIRE CHEESE FACTORY is on the way to the Museum along the Point Reyes-Petaluma Road, just 9 miles northeast of Point Reyes Station. They make cheese in the old European style: *brie, camembert, schloss* and others. Tours of the cheese-making area are available. Call ahead for information (707) 762-6001.

©1995 Ane Rovetta

About Chardon Press

Founded in 1988 by Kim Klein and Nancy Adess, Chardon Press publishes works relating to or funding the work of social justice and social change.

On Fundraising

Grassroots Fundingraising Journal
(6 issues annually)

Grassroots Grants: An activist's Guide to Proposal Writing
Andy Robinson (1996)

Fundraising for Social Change, Third Edition
Kim Klein (1995)

General Interest

Volver a Vivir/Return to Life
PROJIMO/Suzanne Levine, ed. (1996)

Countering the Right: Strategies of Liberation
Suzanne Pharr (1996)

Naming the Truth: Stories of Loretto Women
Ann Patrick Ware, ed. (1995)

Homophobia, A Weapon of Sexism
Suzanne Pharr (1988)

Home on the Range: Recipes from the Point Reyes Community
Forward by Ed Brown (1988)

CHARDON PRESS

P.O. Box 11607
Berkeley, California 94712